I Have Plans for Your Life...

God

MARGUERITE WAFULA

authorHOUSE®

AuthorHouse™
1663 Liberty Drive
Bloomington, IN 47403
www.authorhouse.com
Phone: 1 (800) 839-8640

Published by AuthorHouse 07/14/2020

ISBN: 978-1-7283-6656-2 (sc)
ISBN: 978-1-7283-6654-8 (hc)
ISBN: 978-1-7283-6655-5 (e)

Library of Congress Control Number: 2020912886

Print information available on the last page.

Contents

Contents

Introduction

God sent His Only Son, Jesus Christ into the world to redeem man's relationship and broken fellowship through sin. The sin of one man (Adam) transgressed to all men (humanity). God's redemption plan demanded a sacrificial offering to forgive the offense. Jesus Christ is that offering for all mankind. Through His body and blood, God has forgiven every man and offers an Era of Grace (Dispensation) for all men to have chance to repent and receive salvation. Because of Jesus, it is now possible for every individual to live out the plan God originally intended!

Romans 5:12 NIV, "Therefore, just as through one man's sin entered the world, and death through sin, and thus death spread to all men because all sinned."

First man God created was called Adam, who had transgressed (disobeyed) against God in the Garden of Eden, thereby bringing sin into the world. Every person born now has a fallen (sin) nature. The reason being, since Adam and his wife Eve, had no children prior to this, sin was in every man through birth. Before Adam sinned, there was no sin, sickness, or death. Adam and Eve shared perfect unhindered relationship and fellowship with God, the Creator! The explanation of why today, people sin, and there is sickness everywhere! Prior to this again, there was no such thing! The death that follows sin is physical death and spiritual death, the separation of the self from God by an act of disobedience. As a final outcome, eternal death, or Hell.

Romans 6:23 NIV, "For the wages of sin is death, but the gift of God is eternal life in Christ Jesus our Lord."

My purpose for writing this book is to reveal the true nature of God and expose the lies of the devil. Most if not all, have thought or do think, that God is angry at them, non-caring of their conditions, and unresponsive or unmerciful to do anything to help in their situations! My intention is to encourage you to open your heart and mind to the true living God of the Bible and walk in fellowship with Him! Questioning if the negative comments you've heard about God are accurate? To dare to embrace truths of His word! If you can, I believe dreams will awaken in you left dormant for years; some will begin to dream, and others will remember the visions that God had placed in your heart an exceptionally long time ago! But more than the dreams, goals, and plans, however wonderful they are, I am hopeful, you will begin to know how infinitely and unconditionally God's love for you! To understand with all of your heart, how God wants a relationship and fellowship with you! He is not counting your wrong doings, failures or how you've disregarded Him. He stands with open arms, wanting you to come home!

Hebrews 4:15,16 AMPC, "For we do not have a High Priest who is unable to understand and sympathize and have a shared feeling with our weaknesses and infirmities and liability to the assaults of the temptation, One who has been tempted in every respect as we are, yet without sinning. Let us then fearlessly and confidently and boldly draw near to the throne of grace (the throne of God's unmerited favor to us sinners), that we may receive mercy (for our failures) and find grace to help in good for every need (appropriate help and well-timed help, coming just when we need it)."

Because of the grace and mercy of God and Jesus, He is not angry with us! God is giving us time in this era to repent and turn back to Him! God so loves you! He created you out of that love and always planned **Good** for you! God doesn't have a bad thought towards you! Why, again because of His Son! In other words, Jesus came to make atonement or to pay the penalty for our sins, so that we might be saved.

John 3:16 AMPC, "For God so greatly loved and dearly prized the world that He [even] gave up His only begotten (unique) Son, so that whoever believes in (trusts in, clings to, relies on) Him shall not perish (come to destruction, be lost) but have eternal (everlasting) life."

This means even though, man crucified Jesus at Calvary, God has forgiven man of every past, present and future sins. Why, because Jesus became our living sacrifice, taking the punishment meant for us, to satisfy God's wrath! We owe Jesus a lot but can never repay Him! One day judgment will come to all those who reject the gift of salvation through God's Son! If you reject someone's gift, then nothing has changed! Therefore, the Giver withdraws the gift and the offer, and you remain in your situation! You have been given time to repent and turn back to God before you die in this life! The scriptures say, after death, the judgment!

John 14:6, NLT "Jesus said, I am the way, the truth, and the life, "No one comes to the Father except through Me."

Jesus is the only way to have salvation and a personal relationship with God. Jesus is the mediator between God and man. The only access to God. If you deny God's Son, you deny God, because God sent Him!

John 17:8 NKJV "For I have given to them the words which You have given Me; and they have received them and known surely that I came forth from You; and they have believed that You sent Me ".

This book is about the redemption plan of God revealed through His word, and the Bible! Redemption is the action of saving or being saved from sin, error or evil. God is Holy, meaning exalted or worthy of complete devotion as one perfect in goodness and righteousness. Sin is an immoral act considered to be a transgression against divine law, which is punishable by death. Therefore, man needed a savior and through Jesus Christ, we have not only the Savior but another splendid chance to receive the promises of God and live out His plan for our life! Thank God for His grace and mercy! Amen! God always had and still has a perfect plan for your life and that of mankind. God's heart and plan for you is depicted magnificently in this verse:

Jeremiah 29:11 NKJV, "For I know the thoughts (plans) that I think toward you, says the Lord, thoughts of peace and not of evil, to give you a future and a hope (expected end)."

God has a good end in mind for you. God sees the end before the beginning. He wants your life to be filled with good things; peaceful and hopeful! He is always thinking good of you!

In the book of *Genesis 6:5 NKJV, "Then the Lord saw that the wickedness of man was great in the earth, and that every intent of the thoughts of his heart was only evil continually."* So, we see the contrast here that man can think evil continually, but God is not evil, nor does He think evil about you. His covenant with Jesus was to always bless you! God hasn't changed His mind about why He created you! He wants to bring you back to the purpose of the Garden of Eden!

Chapter 1

What's Your Story?

Everyone has a story, a beginning, a testimony, and your story is unique than anyone else's! God perfectly designed you to be absolutely original! Our stories are similar in the sense, we all have been through heartache, pain, rejection, good times and bad. But we don't all have the same family or live in the same location. No two lives are exactly the same because no two people are exactly the same, not even twins. The world is attempting to replicate man in the form of cloning but only God is the Creator and He has made every person uniquely different. Cloning will never equal nor surpass the intelligent design and intricate details of God's creation! What makes you so special? In the eyes of God, He cares about every detail of your life! God never created you to go through hardship or heartache but only to a good life everlasting!

Psalms 139:13-16 NIV, "For you created my inmost being;
you knit me together in my mother's womb.
14 *I praise you because I am fearfully and wonderfully made;*
your works are wonderful,
I know that full well.
15 *My frame was not hidden from you*

when I was made in the secret place,

when I was woven together in the depths of the earth.

16 *Your eyes saw my unformed body;*

all the days ordained for me were written in your book

before one of them came to be."

Your life consists of either a job, a business or maybe retirement. You have interests and activities, particularly outside your work, which make your life enjoyable and worthwhile. In most cases, there are some family members. But as a human race, we all like to feel connected to somebody. When people feel isolated from others, this may cause depression and, in some cases, suicide. This is why you see orphaned children go through a lot of trauma in their lives. They may feel abandoned or not belonging. Even a happy well-adjusted adopted child, wonders about their (real) parents from time to time. Some go as far as to seek them out. This is because God, our Creator, designed us to be together. It's in the genes!

There is a popular company that claim to have a high percentage of accuracy to help individuals find their roots, called Ancestry, where you are encouraged to take an ancestry DNA test and find out where you really come from. An AncestryDNA test is simple, or so I'm told. You order a kit, send in your saliva sample, and voila. You get an email weeks later telling you when your results are ready. Those results reveal your ethnicity estimate, people you may be related to, and new details about your unique family history.

Those tests may be accurate, (I have never tried them), and it would be interesting and maybe good to see how far ones roots traced back. But in actually, the Bible is the most accurate resource that traces as far back to the beginning of time! It tells us our story as a human race, our history, and our roots! That God created the first man, Adam and then his helpmate (wife), Eve, the first woman. God told them to be fruitful and multiply; fill the earth.

We learn from this; that all races (human) came out of Adam. Even Eve came out of Adam.

Genesis 2:7NKJV, "And the Lord God formed man of the dust of the ground."

Genesis 2:21, 22 NKJV, "And the Lord God caused a deep sleep to fall on Adam, and he slept; and He took one of his ribs and close up the flesh in its place. Then the rib which the Lord God had taken from the man, He made into a woman, and He brought her to the man."

Every race, cultures of languages and nation, came out of the seed of Adam! This is how the world began and begin to populate. However, your personal life story started, God has destined you for greatness! He did not create you to fail and be clueless about what He has provided for you! God created you to know Him! There is hope for your situation. Your future would look so bright if you could only see through the eyes of the Creator!

It is important, to picture yourself as valuable or worthwhile to

God, because you are! He foresaw you before your conception. His plan has always been to give you a hope and a future. Adam, and Eve, are examples of God's original intent for mankind. They were given the same free will we all have. The same right and ability to choose to reject God or obey Him. God is not a dictator, nor does He want us to be robotic and a puppet. But the greatest attribute of His nature is love; and that love allows you to choose, even to reject Him. Adam, and Eve made the wrong decision, as we do so often today; God who is rich in mercy and grace, forgave them and gave them another chance. He is giving us another chance! If someone offers you a pardon, then you reject the offer and proceed to blame the giver for your problems that arose after you refused the gift, that's insanity! We can no more blame God for our choices, than we can for the consequences that is a result of our actions. God is not controlling us and if He were to, we would not like it.

In America, we enjoy a lot of freedoms but if someone were to take our rights and control us, we would protest. God created us to have freedoms to think and make good choices! And when we succeed, it is our human nature, to not want to be told what to do. If we fail, then we want to blame someone else. This wrong mindset is a result of sin and our fallen nature from birth. Adam and Eve first played the blame game in the beginning. There is nothing new under the sun, the Bible tells us, and it is so true! When they sinned, God came to judge them and Adam blamed God for the woman and Eve, saying the wife you gave me, did this. Eve turned around and blamed the serpent, saying he deceived her! We must take ownership and be accountable for our actions. No matter how much you fail, God is on your side. He is your #1 supporter, cheering you on and believing in you!

Romans 5:8 NKJV, "But God demonstrates his own love for us in this: While we were still sinners, Christ died for us."

After salvation, some believers are left wondering what's next. Are they simply to attend church regularly and wait to go to heaven? Perhaps they weren't taught what the Bible says about living the Christian life, or they may have never considered what God desires for them as His children. But by reading Scripture, believers can discover that God has plans that He desires to work out in their lives today.

My story or life with Christ began 48 years ago asking the Lord Jesus to come in to my heart and life! I was a child, but I knew there had to be more than just asking, then what? Soon after, prayer became a habit for me; talking to God and our family attended church regularly. Reading the Bible was not an understanding I had, although. And basically, I was a loner, who was content with few friends and family. Consequently, I knew little about who God was. Whenever circumstances would become worrisome for me, I would talk to God about it. Praying a lot gave me solace but there was no understanding on how to get my prayers answered. It was very one-sided conversations to me. My high expectations were for God to also speak to me.

A fervent prayer request of mine from my teenage years, was for God to send me a good husband. As the years went by into my adulthood, and the more I learned through my local pastor's teachings on marriage and relationship, my request was for me to be a good wife also! I wanted lots of children, but I do not recall praying as much for the children, even though it was a desire. It was interesting, however, for a long time and on many occasions, I would get disappointed with God, after no responses from Him. I wondered was He listening or was indifferent.

John 3:3 AMPC, "Jesus answered him, "I assure you and most solemnly say to you, unless a person is born again [reborn from above—spiritually transformed, renewed, sanctified], he cannot [ever] see and experience the kingdom of God."

There is a great misunderstanding of what it means to be born again! This scripture is not referring to the flesh and blood physical birth where you are born through your mother's womb, but you are born again, spiritually. Where God comes to dwell within you (as you ask) by His Spirit. At this conversion, the Holy Spirit baptizes the now Believer into the Body of Christ! This is what is called the Body of Christ, the Church! In other words, God is a spirit and He created us in His likeness.

The first man, Adam, was not living until God breathed his Spirit of life in him. The Bible says he became a living being. Likewise, each person is a spirit and we have a body, the flesh. We live because God's life is in our bodies. Without His life or spirit, we will die. What fell when Adam sinned was his nature and thus our nature after him and his flesh began to age. Before the fall, Adam and Eve's flesh were perfect and they would have lived forever in that state. So, would we, when we were born. After the fall, their nature was no longer like God's but sinful. So, the body, if we don't bathe, we smell and why every day we age grow older, we celebrate another year's birthday! When man fell, he died spiritually and through the process of time, physically. When we receive Jesus, we are given God's nature again and His Spirit comes to live or remain in us.

When you receive Jesus Christ into your heart, it opens up the door for God to manifest all His blessing He has for you because of His Goodness and the finished work of the cross of Jesus! After speaking those heartfelt words, without this understanding, nothing to you will have seemed to have changed on the outside, and it doesn't, you look the same. If you were 10 lbs. overweight before, you will still be overweight. If you had an addiction, you could have received your deliverance at the same time receiving salvation but spiritually, you have been set free! But if you don't receive deliverance, where the desire for the addiction has left you immediately, you will still have the same problem, but you will be born-again. What changed was on the inside! Your spirit is born-again of God and you now have the nature of God! What needs to take place now, is 'renewing of your mind', to what you have received. This only comes through reading and studying the word of God, the Bible and allowing God by His Spirit to teach you!

No matter where you were born and raised; no matter the walks of life you've encountered; no matter who your parents are or your talents and interests may be, the word of God tells us it is God who created you and knew you before you ever came to be. Before your parents conceived you, He saw you and planned to prosper you, for it pleases Him to do so!

The restoration of a relationship with mankind lost after the first man, Adam, sinned! The Bible tells us in *Genesis 3:8 that Adam heard the sound of the Lord God walking in the garden in the cool of the day.* But in order for something to be restored or mended back together again, there had to been a focal point, where it all began.

We as a human race, have the same story. God created us but not with shattered lives. He created us perfectly, lacking nothing. This all changed because the world is fallen, and we are born in sin. We need to be born-again. And individually we all have a history, of how things began. God never compares your past to see how your future will be, but your past has answers.

Many of us either attended a local church from time to time or grew up going to church on a regular basis mostly with some family members. We can attest to the pastor preaching each time of the cross and a man named Jesus who died on the cross for our sins! If you were like me, I could picture Jesus on the Cross and I took by faith He died for my sins. There was some understanding of the significance of why Jesus had to die. But what happened after the Cross; after the Resurrection and the true importance was never taught! One person stated to me, it is as if Jesus was still on the Cross!

Sounds funny, but seriously, some live their lives as if God and Jesus can do something but that they have done nothing! By faith, you believe Jesus has died for your sins and you make the decision to receive Jesus in your heart and life, but you don't realize the benefits and privileges you now have! What a truly momentous occasion! But I knew it was so much more. Not that salvation is totally awesome and gracious of God by itself. Thank God there is so much more!!

Again, childhood experiences can be similar or different, but most people have the same three questions: 1) Why I am here? 2) Who is God? and 3) What is my purpose in life? After all, this is religion, man trying to reach God, to see who He really is!

Some of us become regular church goers. Somehow believing the more we attend or stay in church, the closer we are to God and it helps us to feel good about ourselves. While others, choose to stay away from the church all together or most of the time, only visiting on special occasions like Christmas, Easter, or Mother's Day. You may not find any interests in church or purpose to going or could be running from God. Even to the point of being angry with Him for an imagined wrong He has done. We may serve in the church as an usher or on the choir, very sincerely but can be done without knowing your real potential or purpose in life. Some are in positions or callings; God did not tell you to be in! Maybe you read your Bible faithfully, but it is just religion or a ritual, for you have no real relationship with the living God! If you are not truly born again, you are not saved, going to church regularly or being a longtime member is not salvation. Just because you go to church doesn't mean you're a Christian. I can go sit in the garage all day and it doesn't make me a car. The Bible tells us we must be born again!

Reading the Bible on a daily basis is awesome but we can read with no understanding or idea of the application of the word in our everyday lives. We can form our own rituals that become important to us but without proper understanding of how this relates to God, can be fruitless to you! Doing all these things are good but alone, will not save you! Only receiving the blood and bodily sacrifice of Jesus can save you!

Religion can be a life-filled deception! *Hosea 4:6 AMPC, "My people are destroyed for lack of knowledge."* Religion is trying to reach God and chase Him, but truth is God is chasing you and He wants your heart in a relationship with Him. God is a relational God. He created man to fellowship and worship Him. All the laws of the Ten Commandments hang on two, love the Lord God with all your heart, soul and mind and love others! We were not created to be alone or separate ourselves but to help, serve and love each other!

If God can have your heart, He will get your service. Christianity is relationship with God. Reading the Bible, attending church, and praying, are all byproducts of that relationship. You're not doing these things to be saved but because you are already saved, it makes you want to do these things.

Out of the abundance of your heart, your actions will follow. This is why God says, if you seek Him first and His ways of doing things, everything else, every concern, your service will be added. For example, in a good human relationship, if the persons involved are receiving all they need from the other, it is easier to relate to that person. It is easier to be kind, loving, returning good to them!

Matthew 6:33NIV, "But seek first his kingdom and his righteousness, and all these things will be given to you as well."

Because God desires relationship with you, He tells us to draw closer to Him and He will draw closer to you. A lot of people think God is in control of everything and it can be understandable why they may think this due to the fact; God is Holy! The problem with this reasoning, is it leaves man out of the equation of participating! Yes, God is in control in the sense He is Creator, and everything belongs to Him. He is Sovereign and there is no one equal, nor comparable to Him! He is the top of the chain as they say! But God, chose to create man with the ability to reason and have a free will! We have the right to choose and God will honor that decision we make, whether to our perishing or to everlasting life; all the while making it clear, He wants us to choose life! We have a part to play in life, given to us by God Himself! So, in this aspect God is certainly not controlling our free will!

We see this in scriptures so often where God tells us to choose this day who you will serve, let not your heart be troubled, pray without ceasing to name a few! It is up to the individual whether he obeys the commandment or not. While surely, there are consequences to our actions, but it is still your decision.

Seeking God and who He is; His plans for your life, according to the Bible takes time, prayer, discipline, and faith! The beginning of anything in God has to start with faith. God saw the heavens and the earth and by His faith, said "let there be," and it was so! We have to believe He is God and our faith be in Him before we can have faith to believe the rest of the Bible. Walking with God is a lifestyle of faith not an event, not a marathon. It is a commitment such as you would make with your spouse or a marriage. Falling down, you get back up, messing up, you repent and start again purposing to do better the next time. This is the life with God. He knows our frame and if we try, He will help us to succeed!

Whatever your story or beginning, the starting point of a relationship and fellowship with God is first to ask Him to come into your heart and life!

Romans 10:9,10 NKJV, "That if you confess with your mouth the Lord Jesus and believe in your heart that God has raised Him from the dead, you will be saved. For with the heart one believes unto righteousness, and with the mouth confession is made unto salvation."

These are the words I and so many countless others have spoken to begin our new life in Christ Jesus! Some may want to get to God by another person or being, like Buddha, Mohammed, or other religion, but those are dead idols and will not help you! It is God who sets the standard and not we ourselves. His ways are right and just and so much higher than ours, therefore; it is not what we think or want but what God demands. The created cannot command anything of the Creator!

Joshua 1:9 NIV, "Have I not commanded you? Be strong and courageous. Do not be afraid; do not be discouraged, for the LORD your God will be with you wherever you go."

Chapter 2

When God Seems Silent

Most if not all of us, can relate to times we have felt God is either not listening or does not care what's going on with us! Some may wonder if He is real and others may ask, where is He, why doesn't He say something? Why doesn't He do something, rather? If you allow yourself to be frustrated, one day, you will just stop trying to know! Seeking God out of your own reasoning and not according to the Bible, will cause you to have a false impression of Him. Forming a false god in your thinking process. As a result, your life will be of chaos and confusion. For you will never have eternal life and true peace without God! And to discover God's plan for your life, will require your reading and studying the word for yourself!

The Bible tells us, it is understandable if when you begin to seek God, you're like a blind person stumbling trying to find your way. The Bible further explains by giving an example of a baby desiring milk only. As the child grows, milk is less needful and as an adult, has appetites for meatier foods! God will take you just as you are, in your childish ways, all broken and a total mess, but He loves you too much to leave you this way! He expects you to mature! From a baby not knowing anything, what to do, how to walk, where to go;

to a point where you learn to stand on your own and be strong and confident in the Lord! And an ever-increasing awareness of who He is and who you are in Christ Jesus! Having an understanding or revelation of what you have in Christ as a Believer!

Ephesians 1:17-19 NKJV, "that the God of our Lord Jesus Christ, the Father of glory, may give to you the spirit of wisdom and revelation in the knowledge of Him, the eyes of your understanding being enlightened; that you may know what is the hope of His calling, what are the riches of the glory of His inheritance in the saints, and what is the exceeding greatness of His power toward us who believe, according to the working of His mighty power."

To have our spiritual eyes open to this revelation is an ongoing process! There is no formula of A to Z steps or suddenly one day you happen to arrive at your destination of knowing everything. On the contrary, as long as you live, until your death, (barring the Rapture) you will need to continue growing in the knowledge and revelation of God's word! So, to coin a popular phrase, "I have not arrived, but I have left!" *Have you left*? Have you taken steps toward seeking who God is and what He desires for your life? God says, move closer towards Him (in your heart) and He will come closer to you!

Soon after receiving Jesus Christ in my heart, I knew I was born again. Inexplainable, unless you have experienced this, but I was just confident about it. I did not look differently on the outside after my confession nor after the water baptism; I went down in the water dry and came up wet! Unbeknownst, I had no insight of the spiritual transformation that took place on the inside of me! I felt drawn now to know this person whom I had committed my life. With baby steps at first, unintentionally I endeavored to know God without reading the Bible. My knowledge was limited to Jesus dying on the Cross for my sins, which I happily accepted.

But one thing I can say, I talked to God a lot! About my problems, about direction, about everything. The highlight of my day was to talk to God! After some time, it became disappointing to me when God was always so silent! This feeling continued for over a decade. There was no impression of any kind of God saying anything to me. I did not realize; I was trying to reach God without His word, which proved to be a big block! One day, God led me to hear a radio broadcast from a local pastor, admonishing confessed Christians who had never read the Bible and challenging the same to read the entire Bible in a year! This was a pivotal point in my life and changed my life for the better! Set me on a path of reading and studying God's word, where today I love expounding on the scriptures and the Holy Spirit has given me a Bible teaching ministry!

The Bible contains the word of God! Every word in the Bible is not what God is saying but includes the testimonies of others! Everything in the Bible is what God wants to be there. The Bible is the inspired word of the living God. Men wrote the Bible moved by the Holy Spirit! There are multitudes of situations and testimonies in the Bible, where God wanted to leave as examples for us to learn from. God does not control the affairs of men nor did He in the Bible with the men and women there. Therefore, not all testimonies are approved by God. For example, Abraham fearing for his own life and self-centeredness, pretended Sarah was not his wife. God did not tell him to do this, nor does God lie or tell others to lie. Another example, King David, murdered a man because he lusted for the man's wife. In order to have her, David had her husband killed. Thus, he too was guilty. Again, God did not approve of this but rather took David's first-born child he conceived with this woman as punishment. God moved on men to have such testimonies in the Bible to teach us a moral lesson, of what to do and not to do.

Could it be, on your quest to know the plan of our life, God is silent to you because you have not read the Bible at all! Or, perhaps, you're not reading on a regular basis? The Old Testament people had God talk to them through a priest or prophet. They did not have a book put together like we do today. Today, we have the Holy Spirit, who speaks to the Believers from our born-again spirits. The Holy Spirit testifies of Jesus. He brings what Jesus says back to your remembrance.

Sadly, today, many are blaming God, attributing tragedies to Him without having ever read the word or are reading with little understanding. As my childlike mannerisms were early in my walk with God, it should not be this way now. As you mature in your reading and studying, you will be in a better position to face the challenges of this world.

I cannot stress enough the importance of studying the Bible! It is a stumbling block if you buy a car with more features than you are accustomed to or buy a gadget where you have no idea how to use; and do not first read the manual. But you expect this same vehicle to serve you well, running smoothly and efficiently for you. You will miss out on some things until you understand what you have. Try putting together furniture with all its nuts and bolts the first time without reading the little how to book first! But it is our human nature, I guess, we try to learn about and know the ways of our Creator without becoming acquainted with the Bible! You can say in a real sense, the Bible is God's chosen instruction manual of His salvation plan. It's our origin and our future! The Bible is the #1 Best Seller of all time and still being sold out today! No other book is as well-known and sought after. On the other hand, no other book is as criticized because if you have heard the analogy, if you throw rocks at a pack of dogs, the one that yells the loudest is the one who got hit! The Bible sears the conscience, bringing conviction and change. Granted in a good way, but the truth will hurt or sting for a while.

Deuteronomy 4:29 NKJV, "But from there you will seek
the Lord your God, and you will find Him if you seek
Him with all your heart and with all your soul."

We are told in His word, God will not continue to be silent to you, if you are seeking Him will all your heart. Your heart has to be involved. It cannot be a ritual or make a wish foundation expectation. God is not going to grant our every wish but only according to His will are the promises in Christ, yes and amen! As we do what the word says to do, God will not be silent to you! He wants His will fulfilled in your life. Most people only reach out to God out of a need at that time, when the need is met, they no longer seek God! When prayers seem to go unanswered, we reason out of our own intellect what God may be saying. Instead of going to the book of answers, the Bible.

James 4:2,3 NKJV," You lust and do not have. You murder and covet and cannot obtain. You fight and war. Yet you do not have because you do not ask. You ask and do not receive, because you ask amiss, that you may spend it on your pleasures."

God could be silent to you because He is not giving you the answer you want. We pray and try to pressure God with our prayer requests along with the help of others joining us, until God answers the way we want. He is not obligated to answer us apart from His nature and according to His will! He wants you to know His will more than you do! We need to remember, God created us to worship Him and fellowship with Him!

God will not tell you anything outside of what He has spoken!

His word is final. In the movie, 'The Ten Commandments', it was often said by Pharaoh, "So let it be written, so let it be done." A decree was made, or law and it could not be changed or altered. Pharaoh decreed to remove Moses from history, and that no one speak of Him ever again. On the deathbed of Pharaoh, because in his heart, he loved Moses, he broke his own law and repeated the name Moses!

But God is not like a human. When God says something, it is done! He cannot take it back or change His mind! If God were able to lie, the whole universe would self-destruct. God created the heavens and the earth. The moon, stars, sea, wind, and the sun, each obey His commands! But the good news is, God cannot lie! You are setting yourself up for disappointment, to ask God for anything outside of His will! On the contrary, getting to know God through His word and receiving what He says, will bring peace and comfort to your soul! It will be well with you! I've observed the poem, 'Sometimes God says yes, sometimes no and sometimes wait. But the scriptures tell us, all the promises of God through Christ are Yes and Amen for the glory of God! They are available right now, 24/7.

Another example, holding a conversation with God where you don't wait for the answer, you plunge ahead saying God said. This is an analogy of how we can relate to God! It is all one sided. We ask and answer the question for Him of what we want the answer to be! Some people wish God would obey everything they say and do whatever they ask. It doesn't work like that! It's like hit and miss.

I found out, as a child, God doesn't have to respond to tantrums, crying or pleading in prayers. The strategy is to get as many people as possible, to storm the gates of heaven praying and provoking God to listen and answer your prayer the way you want. No, God responds every time to FAITH!

Hebrews 11:6 AMP, "But without faith it is impossible to [walk with God and] please Him, for whoever comes [near] to God must [necessarily] believe that God exists and that He rewards those who [earnestly and diligently] seek Him.

Remember God is a spirit, so praying in the spirit is essential to having the power of God flowing in your life! This is another experience you have as a Believer. To worship God is to do so from a sincere heart. God looks at the heart. The scriptures say God is seeking such to worship Him. Seeking God with all of your heart, and you will find Him.

John 4:24 AMP, "God is spirit [the Source of life, yet invisible to mankind], and those who worship Him must worship in spirit and truth."

You're not speaking His language! God is a spirit and we are flesh. When we pray with our spirit to Him, who is Spirit, the communication is much clearer and effective! Praying from your intellect or mind, without the word will not enable you to hear God.

The Baptism of the Holy Spirit

As his child your loving heavenly father wants to give you the supernatural power you need to live this new life.

Luke 11:10,13 NKJV, "For everyone that asks receives; and he who seeks finds; and to him who knocks it shall be opened. If you know how to give good gifts unto your children how much more shall your heavenly Father give the Holy Spirit to them that asks Him."

When you ask, believe, and receive, you're releasing God's power from within and building yourself up in the spirit. It's just that simple but also powerful! This is a gift of God. Many Christians do not have this but I and others that do will testify it is needed to live a more victorious life. Again, you will pray from your spirit to God who is spirit.

The flesh will hinder you. You know when I say, flesh, for example, when you are reading the Bible or praying, how tired you feel. The flesh or your body, is not saved yet. One day we will have glorified bodies but until then the flesh is an enemy of God and the things of God. Your flesh will rise up to tell you in your mind, you are tired and should not read the word or should not pray or should not go to church. The Baptism of the Holy Spirit is a gift from God to effectively communicate with you!

God's silence to you may be one sided. You may not be hearing Him, even though you are talking! God wants you to commune with

Him, more than you do. If Jesus had not have come and conquered sin and death at the cross, we would not have ability to come to God on our own! God has a plan for you but to know this plan, you have to begin taking a step of faith towards Him and simply asking for His help!

To seek means, obviously, that you do not have all the answers. Making these mistakes with God, I had to grow up. As you seek God in life, you will not only make mistakes, but you will learn from them. God wants us to expect Him to do great things in our lives! Seek God until you find Him. Search for Him with all your heart. God says to you to trust Him and the plans He has for you, to bring you an expected end. Expected end means something that has been estimated and projected. He cannot do this without your cooperation.

I've heard some say God is talking all the time. I can't say they are wrong, but my opinion is that according to what we read of the testimonies of the men and women in the Bible, we cannot conclude this!

First, we know God can be silent because the word of God tells us. The 400 Years of Silence is the name given to the period of time between the last of the Old Testament prophets and the arrival of Jesus in the New Testament. The Jews did not live as God instructed. The Jewish Homeland was taken over from the Persians by the Greek empire in 332 BC followed by the Egyptian occupation in 312 BC. The children of Israel became disillusioned and doubted God's provision and their faith was lacking. They began to become cynical and wonder whether it was worth serving God after all. The priests were not obeying God. It was chaos and so God became silent.

With this in mind, I do not believe God is talking all the time either. Particularly if an individual is not listening. Why would God continue to talk if you are being rebellious? When your own children intentionally do not obey you or seem to be an annoyance, you may respond with, "I give up!" Implying the desire to stop talking because your words are being wasted. Why not God who chooses his words very carefully? God does not speak unless it is necessary, I believe. And when He does speak, He means what He says.

Second, why would God talk to us all the time, knowing we could not possibly comprehend in our finite minds, what He is saying every moment. I just don't see this! Maybe God has no new instructions for you. He will speak when there is a need or reason to. Remember, God is allowing us to rule in our world. We have been given freedom to make our own decisions and orchestrate the affairs of our lives to a large extent.

God can be silent but not indifferent. The Bible says, *Psalms 138 :8 NKJV, "The Lord will perfect that which concerns me."* He is not worried or fearful, but cares what concerns I have. This scripture says He is wanting to do something about it! It is been my experiences, that God does not repeat Himself unnecessarily! If He says the same thing more than once, it is to emphasize a point but not to ramble like we do. *Matthew 5:37 NKJV, "But let your 'Yes' be 'Yes,' and your 'No,' 'No,' for whatever is more than these is from the evil one.""* Simply affirming or declaring that a thing is so. Your word is your bond. I remember growing up when a handshake or a spoken promise was stronger than today's legal contracts! God is truth. Our Lord does not enjoin the precise terms wherein we are to affirm or deny, but such a constant regard to truth as would render oaths unnecessary."

A love of the world can cause God to be silent to you, but God is wanting to speak to you! The blockage is on your side.

1 John 2:15, 16 NIV, "Do not love the world or anything in the world. If anyone loves the world, love for the Father is not in them. For everything in the world—the lust of the flesh, the lust of the eyes, and the pride of life—comes not from the Father but from the world."

The cares of the world can make God seem silent to you. The world and this world system are an enmity of God. The kingdom of God and this fallen world are hostile towards one another. They are not the same. In goals, morality, speech, or purpose. The world system is anti-God in every way. It seeks to say the opposite of what God has said. The scripture says, if you love the world, then you cannot love the Father. You don't know Him, so your prayers are hindered or stalled. The cares of the world are typified in the temptation Christ overcame in the wilderness at the end of His fast!

Lust of the flesh - longing or yearning for the flesh. Flesh against the Spirit are contrary to one another. The Bible describes these in Galatians as: adultery, fornication, uncleanness, lewdness, idolatry, sorcery, hatred, contentions, jealousies, outbursts of wrath, selfish, ambitions, discord, heresies (denial of revealed spiritual truths), envy, murders, drunkenness, festivities and the like. The **lust of the flesh** is that temptation to feel physical pleasure from some sinful activity—to **do** something to make the **flesh** feel satisfied. It can involve any type of sinful activity that will bring pleasure to the body. In Luke, Jesus was tempted by satan who came to Him after His forty day fast had ended. Satan knew Jesus was hungry and with hunger comes weakness in the flesh. Hunger symptoms can make you irritable. Satan was counting on this weakness to defeat the Son of God and thereby, our chance for restoration to God would be null and void!

The enemy will tempt you with things that are appealing to your flesh. Brings gratification for a little while but the end is death to you. There is always an attachment to what satan offers. He makes the offer seem unconditional but there are hidden conditions when you accept. The thief (names of the devil and satan) comes only but to steal, kill and to destroy. Just as he deceived Eve in the Garden of Eden with lies, he will do the same to you. He did not come to Eve shouting or commanding, but the Bible tells us he came through the most beautiful creature at that time, crafty and convincing! Tricked her out of her divine authority, blessings, dominion, power, and relationship with God!

The reason for fasting is not to twist God's arms (figuratively), into doing something for you but to bring the body (flesh) into subjection (dominion to your will). Jesus fasted, bringing His body into subjection to the will of the Father, so when satan showed up, Jesus flesh was not in charge but His will! God can seem silent to you because your flesh could be the factor. It is not God's will who wants this but according to your decision.

Lust of the eyes - is the desire to possess what we see or to have those things which have visual appeal. The Bible describes these as coveting (yearn to possess or have (something). Such as money, someone's wife or husband, a house owned by someone else, a ministry not divinely given to you, status, someone's clothes, or anything belonging to someone else. Part of the reason Eve listened to the serpent in the Garden was that she *looked* at the forbidden fruit and saw that it was "pleasing to the eye" Satan used a visual image to help entrap her. Satan tried a similar tactic on Jesus. One of his temptations in the wilderness was an attempt to make Jesus covet earthly power. Satan used a visual: he "showed him all the kingdoms of the world and their splendor. He then promised to give them to Jesus. The price was for Jesus to worship him. There is always a price with satan, but you will not know the full contract of the agreement going into the deal. Of course, Jesus did not succumb to the lust of the eyes, and Satan was defeated. We should follow Jesus' example and, in the power of the Holy Spirit, resist the enemy!

The world is full of "eye candy," glamor, and gaudiness, that promises happiness and fulfillment. You cannot watch a program on television without commercials advertising and glamourizing of sickness and disease. People are being desensitized to the healing power of God! Carrying around oxygen tanks and oxygen through your nose is the normal. Even social distancing is classified as the 'new normal.' It is the new normal to the world but not to God and should not be to His children! What God offers is far better than sickness and defeat, but He promises healing and prosperity. We must not yield to the tricks of the enemy. All that glitters is not gold, and the child of God must know that fame and fortune, quickly fade. Today, if you say anything contrary to the world, a Christian is considered hating people and not accepting all people! We are not to accept the behaviors and lifestyle of all people as normal, particularly in the light of God's instruction in His word!

Living a life outside of the boundaries of God's guidelines, and then trying to fit God into your plan, will cause God to seem silent to you! He will not hear you! He will turn a deaf ear.

Pride of life - The pride of life can be defined as anything that leads to arrogance, flamboyance, pride in self, opinionated, and boasting. John makes it clear that these things are of the world, and the love of the Father is not in him. You see a pattern here from the enemy is, he has no new tricks but just tempts different people with the same temptations. The two examples used again are with Eve which occurs in the Garden of Eden, where Eve was tempted by the serpent to disobey God and eat the forbidden fruit from the tree of the knowledge of good and evil. Eve perceived that the fruit was desirable for gaining wisdom. Eve perceived the fruit would make her wise, giving her wisdom beyond her own. Part of Satan's lie was that eating the fruit would make her "like God, knowing good and evil. She was already like God in His image and she and Adam lacked nothing! Satan's lie told Eve God was holding out on her or keeping something back from her. The only thing God was wanting to 'keep from her and every person,' was the knowledge of good and evil. Which they did not need to know. God only wanted her to know Him, Goodness! Anything that exalts us above God in any way, such as knowledge, status, or wisdom is arrogance!

The temptation with Christ in the wilderness was satan trying to get Jesus to be out of the will of the Father or His plan for the redemption of mankind. Thank God, Jesus did not succumb to this trickery! This attitude and rebelliousness were the very sin which resulted in Satan's expulsion from heaven and doomed his fate. He desired to be God, not to be a servant of God. This arrogant boasting is the root cause of strife in families, churches, and nations. It is exalting self and God clearly distains pride. When we exalt ourselves above God, we can expect God to seem silent to us! But when we obey and follow God's instructions, we can expect God out of relationship and fellowship to speak to our hearts!

Chapter 3

I Am A Child of God!

On your journey seeking God and knowing what He desires of your life, you will read and hopefully come to receive who you are in Christ Jesus! And what God accomplished through the finished work of the Cross of Jesus for you! This is a point that bears repeating; even the richest and most prosperous person in this life, without Jesus is damned in the next life! It is absolutely essential you have a revelation of the love of God that would inspire Him to go to the cross for you!

There are 2 powerful prayers in the book of Ephesians, I would like to point out. First, regarding a *Prayer of Realization* of the love of God!

Ephesians 3:16-19 NIV, "I pray that out of his glorious riches he may strengthen you with power through his Spirit in your inner being, 17 so that Christ may dwell in your hearts through faith. And I pray that you, being rooted and established in love, 18 may have power, together with all the Lord's holy people, to grasp how wide and long and high and deep is the love of Christ, 19 and to know this love that surpasses knowledge – that you may be filled to the measure of all the fullness of God."

This is a prayer for you to have inner strength, the ability to comprehend what you have obtained in Christ and what is going on in your heart. To have the knowledge of God's deep love and His strength. The revelation of His Spirit dwelling or living on the inside of you. The Holy Spirit is a gift from God for us to be used! We are most blessed, when we know others are satisfied with a gift, we have given them! The Holy Spirit was sent to help us live victorious lives! God sent the best because He knew what we needed! God is the Best!

Because God loves you, He sent the same Spirit that raised Jesus from the dead! The same power it took (Resurrection Power) to raise Jesus from the dead lives on the inside of every Believer, working on your behalf! We have overcoming power ready at our disposal! God loves you beyond your comprehension! The greatest challenges or obstacles in your life, has no power over you! Have you ever been so much in love, that the returned love of that person means everything to you! You feel there is nothing you can't handle because that person loves you. That feeling and deep love comforts your heart and soul! You feel strengthened and can take on whatever the world throws at you. When you increase in receiving the love of God, nothing the world throws at you can take away your joy and peace. For joy and peace did not come through the world and the world cannot take it away. Remember that song with similar lyrics? It's true! Someone once told me, "Life is good." I guess they were having a good day and I was glad for them. My reply was, "God is better!" Life in this fallen world can bring good days and not so good, depending on your perspective and responses but God is Good all the time! What a day brings does not compare to the experience of knowing no matter what, God loves me. Through all my faults, failures, and attitudes I know God loves me. He is more than the whole world against me! Realizing someone loves me like that, who is constant and does not change their opinion and loves me unconditionally, days pass but God is eternal!

So many people are deceived concerning God's love for them. For all they really have is head knowledge or just a ritual going to church. The scripture states to be filled with the fullness of God. How can you be filled in the fullness of God? To become rooted and confident in His love by spending time with the one who first loved you! It is called a relationship! You do this, by reading what God says and believing and then receiving by faith. Your faith will increase over the process of time. Joy and peace will begin to fill your heart and then spill into other parts of your life to others! God wants you to understand and experience the goodness of His love for you!

John 3:10, NIV: "You are Israel's teacher,' said Jesus, 'and do you not understand these things?"

Jesus was talking to Nicodemus, explaining to him about spiritual birth and assuring him, "You must be born again." Jesus gave examples of the wind blowing comparing to the Spirit; you hear the sound of it but cannot tell where it comes or goes. Whoever is born of the Spirit has the spirit birth on the inside. Nicodemus was a teacher of Israel. He knew the scriptures frontwards and backwards, inside, and out. The Jewish leaders were required to know the scriptures and laws, but Jesus told Nicodemus, he had truly little understanding of the things of God!

The scriptures will seem like foolishness to you without the Holy Spirit giving you revelation! Like Nicodemus, we may read the Bible but with little understanding. There is a difference between quoting, memorizing and revelation! As a Children's Church teacher, the children were required to learn memory bible verses. A memory verse is just knowledge unless you allow the Spirit of God to reveal to you it's meaning! To bring to life the word of God poured out into your heart!

Praying vain repetitious prayers. Jesus spoke about this:

Matthew 6:7 NKJV, "And when you pray, do not use vain repetitions as the heathen do. for they think that they will be heard for their many words."

God is looking at your heart, to see if whether you are sincere or just repeating yourself with no real heart involved in the prayers addressed to Him or the prayer in general. The heathen He is speaking of in this scripture, are those who do not have a relationship with God, do not know Him nor care about the things He cares about. Prayer can become just formality; something you do without your heart involved. So, when we act like the unbelievers, there is no difference. There should be because you say you're a Christian.

Jesus wants all of you! Your heart is the real you and your actions will follow your heart! It bears repeating, God does not want robots, but human beings. He created you to feel, to reason and be engaged!

It is equally essential for you to have a realization what you have in Christ Jesus as a Believer! Lack of knowledge is costly and in fact, God says, "My people are destroyed for lack of knowledge." We can live defeated lives, or we can live victorious lives as Christians. On our way to heaven, saved and loved by God but the difference in this life what you will receive from God, is your knowledge of Him and what He desires for your life!

Ephesians 1:16-20 NIV, "I have not stopped giving thanks for you, remembering you in my prayers. [17] I keep asking that the God of our Lord Jesus Christ, the glorious Father, may give you the Spirit of wisdom and revelation, so that you may know him better. [18] I pray that the eyes of your heart may be enlightened in order that you may know the hope to which he has called you, the riches of his glorious inheritance in his holy people, [19] and his incomparably great power for us who believe. That power is the same as the mighty strength [20] he exerted when he raised Christ from the dead and seated him at his right hand in the heavenly realms."

Second, this is a *Prayer of Revelation*. For Believers to pray over themselves and others. It is a prayer for eyes opened and enlightened (educated) to know God better! That you would understand the hope you have been called to and of your inheritance! That the same power that it took for God to raise Jesus from the dead, resurrection power, is in every Believer!

God paints a picture of who you now are in Christ Jesus after being born again in the book of *Ephesians, Chapter 1*. The chapter starts out talking about your position in Christ, a position of victory and you already have everything you need to walk this victory out. A Believer is to stand knowing their position no matter what opposition comes to talk them out of it or take it from them! The enemy cannot trick or bully you into believing a lie if you are confident of what you have and whose you belong to! The Bible tells us we have every spiritual blessing available to us through Christ and we are seated in those places of victory. Everything is subject to and under the feet of Christ and since we abide in Him spiritually, everything is under our feet as well! Now that is Good News!

In the verses of Ephesians, Chapter 1, we further look at our position and how we are victorious!

Chosen by the Father

Chosen means to select, pick, or decide. We have been adopted or picked to be in the Family of God; chosen on purpose as an orphan and that this pleases Him to do so! This is what He wants! Sin could not eradicate it, nor a fallen world wash away God selecting you to be born.

Everyone is chosen to receive the blessing of God because it has been revealed to us in the book of Genesis, where God made a covenant with Adam and blessed Him! Thereby, making a covenant with mankind through Adam. God saw you and decided He wanted a relationship with you. Then He decided to create you. When God saw you, He purposed to bless you, lacking nothing! You are not a mistake, accident, or afterthought in the mind of God! You were chosen before the foundations of the world, in which He created!

It is the will of the Father, no one perishes but individuals are perishing every day because of their own free will. God gets glory when we receive His grace, the Bible tells us, He has accepted us when we receive the gift of His Son, Jesus Christ! God has chosen us, but we can decide to choose Him in return!

Redeemed by the Son

We have been redeemed by the blood of Jesus! To redeem means to: compensate for the faults or bad aspects of (something). To gain or regain possession of (something) in exchange for payment. Mankind or humans were lost due to falling into sin or disobedience to God! God sent His Son to regain us back and the exchange was Jesus body and His blood! The payment; His death for our lives! Jesus willingly and not without great sacrifice gave Himself for us! Without Jesus agreeing to come and go to the Cross, to die and take our places (for we deserved the punishment), we would have no hope or access to God or anything He has. We would have no privileges or promises. No covenant or benefits of blessings! We owe Jesus a lot!

Jesus took our sin and sicknesses and anything that would hinder us from God's best! When they whipped Him with lashes, He was receiving our healing! *Isaiah 53:5, "By Jesus stripes, we are healed."* When they chastised Him or scolded Him, He was carrying our peace! The Bible tells us He was led as a sheep to the shearer, but He opened not His mouth! Never complaining but being silent so we would have chance to be reconciled back to the Father. Jesus also gave His blood so we may have forgiveness of sin. Before Jesus, God required offerings of animal sacrifices for the sins of the peoples, but these sacrifices could never atone or correct the wrong doing of mankind and reconcile us back to God! God accepting the sacrifice of Jesus stating:

Ephesians 1:6 NKJV, "He made us accepted in the Beloved." In Matthew 3:17, God characterizes Jesus as His Beloved Son! God accepted His Son's sacrifice and so anyone receiving Jesus is accepted by God! If you reject Jesus, you are rejecting God too! They whipped and pierced Jesus with their spears in His side. This is incredibly significant.

God required animal sacrifices to provide a temporary covering of sins and to foreshadow the perfect and complete sacrifice of Jesus Christ (*Leviticus 4:35, 5:10*). Animal sacrifice is an important theme found throughout Scripture because "without the shedding of blood there is no forgiveness". Adam and Eve sinned; animals were killed by God to provide clothing for them (*Genesis 3:21*). Cain and Abel brought sacrifices to the Lord. Cain's was unacceptable because he brought fruit, while Abel's was acceptable because it was the "firstborn of his flock" (*Genesis 4:4-5*). After the flood receded, Noah sacrificed animals to God (*Genesis 8:20-21*). Jesus is our sacrificial Lamb of God!

Hebrews 9:22 NKJV, "And according to the law almost all things are purified with blood and without shedding of blood there is no forgiveness of sin."

An Inheritance

As Jesus is, so are we in this world! Because of the heart of God and His grace, Jesus is referred to as our brother. God is the Father and everything the Son is entitled to, we as children of God, are entitled to the exact same! As children of God, we are His heirs. Much like an earthly father leaves his children an inheritance, our heavenly Father bestows upon us an inheritance as well. But there is one major condition… we must be His child. We must be born again into His family and pick up our cross to follow Him no matter what the cost. We surrender our hearts to Him in all things, and we allow the Holy Spirit to lead and guide our lives.

We are joint heirs with Christ! Romans 8:16-17 NKJV, "*The Spirit Himself testifies with our spirit that we are children of God, and if children, heirs also, heirs of God and fellow heirs with Christ, if indeed we suffer with Him so that we may also be glorified with Him.*"

We share in His life; we die to sin and our old selves and raise to new life in Him. In sharing in His sufferings, we will also share in His inheritance. What belongs to Jesus will belong to us as children of God. Even more, the Bible tells us even more.

This inheritance is imperishable, undefiled, and will never fade. It is also "reserved in heaven."

Sealed by the Spirit

The word tells us after being born-again, we are guaranteed vacuum packed sealed by the Holy Spirit to keep us from being lost again. And that the Holy Spirit is the guarantee of our inheritance. God is able to keep you if you want to be kept. You can walk away and reject Him, and He will let you go if He sees you really mean it in your heart. But He will never leave you nor forsake you!

The prayer of revelation is that the Believer will come to know and recognize all these benefits and more, you now have because you have received Jesus Christ as your Lord and Savior! This prayer is so we will know our full potential in Christ; having a full revelation of what God has invested in us! So, we have position of victory, adoption, authority, redemption, resurrection empowerment and the forgiveness of sin! And eternal life! But this is only for the Believer. God will bless you anyway because He has compassion on you, but God has commanded His blessings over the His children!

Covenant

God has a covenant with Jesus commanding the blessing over you!

Isaiah 54:10,11 NKJV, "For the mountains shall depart and the hills be removed, but my kindness shall not depart from you, nor shall my covenant of peace be removed, Says the Lord, who has mercy on you."

The kindness of God is expressed through Jesus, when God raised Jesus from the dead, signifying the acceptance of His Son's sacrifice for us! God says He will always show kindness to us. The proof of that is the Covenant He made with Jesus! Again, the book of Ephesians prays we will know this through His love! The width of that love; the length, depth, and height of God's devotion to see you have victory over sin, death and the enemy and reign in life! That God has gone to any means possible making every effort, ensuring you do not perish but having His best!

We have everything we need in this life and eternity because of Jesus but without Christ, we have at best borrowed time in this earth. You do not know your day nor hour you will leave this world or how, but the word tells us, after death, the judgment. You will not get another chance, or your loved ones left behind cannot pay for you and prayers get you into heaven after death. This is it; this is not a dress rehearsal. Maybe, they do so, because they are not sure if their dead loved one made it into heaven. You can be sure of your decision to follow Christ. There is only one payment accepted by God and that is the finished work of the Cross of His Son! There is not another payment God will recognize. You were not worthy to go to the cross yourself, if you were, God would have sent you, but no one was worthy except His Son!

We have so much more in this spiritual benefit package of Christ's! peace even in challenging times, we have confidence toward God. Joy, we cannot explain, from the inside. Not just being happy, for happiness is dependent on circumstances or fleeting; peace and joy are fruit of the spirit. A byproduct of what is already on the inside of the children of God. We have the Holy Spirit and He lives in us, giving us the very nature of God.

We have the promise of the Father to make everything right again and this time, nothing or no one will be able to trick us out of our blessings! Jesus says He has the keys of Hell and Death and *All* authority and power has been given to Him. He shares that power with the Believer!

Oh, bless His Name forever!

In seeking God for His plan for your life, it is good to know what you already have in Christ so that your prayers will be more in line with God's will. When you pray in God's will, He always answers, yes and amen! When you know who you are in the eyes of God, your view of life and circumstances will be viewed in this same light. Your choices will be Christ centered and you will hear God more clearly. I believe maybe Adam and Eve, did not know God as well due to the fact they were created as adults. The Bible does not account for how much time had passed after God created them and when they sinned. They may never have been deceived easily by the enemy and tricked out of their inheritance! It is the truth that you know, that will make you free!

Truth is knowing you are just like God! It is true, we are to approach God as Holy; for He is! We are to reverence, and fear with respect Him! But God, is a living God, who desires to relate to us! Religion is the absence of your heart. You react with no emotions. We are not as animals who God made with instincts, but we can reason and make decisions, plan, create and engage! These attributes come from God! We can love because God is love and created us to love. We laugh and create because this is who God is!

Creativity of millions of inventions that are patented or copyrights of artistic works; all came from our God given abilities! Different expressions of ideas for how to do businesses, is the creativity from the Creator!

Our words have power! God saw and then spoke, "let there be!" Whether it was light, the heavens, and the earth; He spoke everything into existence. We were created with the same power with our words to create. Don't forget, the Bible tells us, God brought Adam (the first man) the animals to name each of them. Not names like a dog named Spotty but the name dog, giraffe, elephant and so on. The names we use to describe what the animal is came from whatever Adam called them! God gave Him power and dominion over the animals.

Have you heard some with green thumbs say, they talk to their plants and they grow and shoot up? Studies and researchers have discovered, what the Bible is saying is true, talking to your plants really can help them grow faster. Power in your words. Your gentle murmurings as you water, trim and feed your plants help it to grow better!

Since these abilities are in every person, how much more, a child of God! We have been blessed with every spiritual blessing! God takes special care of His children! But you can be ignorant of what you already possess by not studying and believing the word of God!

When Abraham Lincoln issued the Emancipation Proclamation, this declared all persons held as slaves, were free. This took time for the slaves to actually go from their slave masters. Some slaves could not read and some of the masters did not want them freed. When they did hear and understand, it still took time for the slaves to move on. Some did not know what they had, and others found it hard to believe. Still others, did not want to go because they were afraid of trying to make it on their own. Slavery was the only life they had known, even if they were treated harshly and cruelly.

So, it is with the renewing of our minds to what we already have received from God through Jesus Christ and the Cross! We cry out to God and when deliverance comes, we can't believe it and are then afraid to move forward out of our comfort zone. Even though, situations are not comfortable, but fear will tell it is better to go backwards.

As a child of God, you are no longer slaves but have been set free from bondage and the chains that held you bound. You can be whatever God tells you to be and go where He sends you. God's children should shine the brightest in a dark world. Being God's masterpiece that He is pleased to show off! There are no limits to what God can and desires to do in your life!

The most important step is to surrender your heart to Jesus Christ and then renew your thinking to who you now are in Christ Jesus! Live a victorious, overcoming life with God as your provider, protector, and defender!

It is quite a contrast when you live your life in relationship to God as a slave verses a child of inheritance! When a royal family member even as a child, are trained for their roles, they walk and talk and hold their heads up high. They know who they are. They know their position in the family and their rights. They know their privileges and wealth!

Hold your head up, child of God, as Jesus is, so are you in this world!

Chapter 4

Please Wait, God is Working

Psalms 121:4 NIV, "He who keeps you shall not slumber nor sleep."

The Lord God who made heaven and earth, keeps you! While we are sleeping, and need to rest, God does not take a nap or doze off on the job! He watches over you and takes care for you while you are asleep. We cannot see or know the countless ways God intervenes on our behalf. Like, sending His angels to guard and protect us! He is forever alert and not subject to needs as humans are*! Proverbs 3:24,* God tells us it is okay to lie down, and your sleep will be sweet. You can trust God to continue working on the plan He has spoken to you as a chicken watches over eggs until they are hatched. As a bird takes care of her babies in the nest.

To say God is working, His timing is not the same as we think. *2 Peter 3:8, tells us with the Lord one day is as a thousand years.* After getting off your knees to pray and before the prayer is answered, we can still be confident that God will answer us. God is not into ignoring people. He wants you to know His will and direction in life. He is the one who started the ball rolling so to speak! He is not going to say, "You're on your own now." God has promised to never abandon us. People will walk away and get tired of you, but God doesn't treat us like people. You can't compare a Holy God to your loved one or neighbor! We have to be patient, as we wait on the Lord, fully trusting Him!

Why did it take Jesus thousands of years to be born of a virgin? Have you ever wondered that? God has given man control of their affairs. In spite of popular belief, He is not controlling our lives like that. He told us to take dominion and subdue the earth. The Believer has authority given to us by Jesus Christ to reign in this life. God had to work through men and their free wills. God can call you to do something for Him and you cannot cooperate or delay and this will cause other factors to arise that were not God's will or in His plan.

There are many examples of this in the Bible. First, God was working through people who cooperated and some who did not. Among whom were prophets, prophetess, and ungodly men who may have hindered the move of God or simply disobedient. God has to work His plan out another way. There are certain events in this world, where God says He will bring to pass. Such as the Rapture of the Church or Believer's or the Second Coming of Christ. There is a permissive will such as given by God to us where we have freedoms, again were God allows. God planned and decreed that Jesus would be born of a virgin and go to the Cross for humanity but the timing of this, would require the involvement of man's will. This is why we are to pray for God's will to be done. If it were automatic, there would be no need for prayer! His will is not always done.

Second, another example, it is the will of God that no one perish, and all come to repentance and be saved. We know, this is not happening, many have perished and more will according to the scriptures. But this is not the desire nor plan of God. Even so, it was not God's will for first couple, Adam, and Eve to disobey Him.

Your will is involved! You have to cooperate with God! He will not force you to do anything. It is good to have an open heart of surrender to follow God wherever He leads you! I've heard some say, they were afraid God would send them to a foreign country as a missionary, so they did not want to hear Him. They blocked their ears and closed their heart. What if God told you to go overseas, would you go, simply because He told you to! To this end, God is working on YOU! You can be the greatest hindrance, not the enemy! God cannot get His plan through you because of your fear, which comes in various forms!

A similar testimony happened to me. I knew according to the plans God was giving me, that God was sending me to foreign missions. I did not know where? I had no preconceived notion of any particular place. I just wanted to go where God wanted me, because I knew where God opens doors, it is a good thing! I could look back and see the times where God was faithful, even in my fears, He came through.

My walk with God led me to trust God more and more with each new trial! I was confident enough in God, that wherever He sent me, He would take care of me and through my experiences, all of them told me, I would not regret following God! My life has been enhanced and taken me to another level each time! This is what it will do for you! The blessings come when you follow God! I do not want to be anywhere but in the will of God!

Therefore, one day, God told me to do missions in Kenya, Africa, and I was totally taken aback! I never considered the continent of Africa in any way. Had never been there before nor had connected with anyone there previously. Looking back, God prepared me before He told me Kenya, Africa before I knew I was being prepared. If God where to tell you too soon, what He had planned for you, we would abort out of fear! He knows our frame. He knows us! Where we came from! Long story short, I journey there, and my life has been enriched beyond my wildest expectations! So grateful!

God is working on you!

Isaiah 40:31 NIV, "But those who wait on the Lord, shall renew their strength; they shall mount up with wings like eagles. They shall run and not be weary, they shall walk and not faint."

Here it is evidently used in the sense of renewing, or causing to revive; to increase, and to restore that which is decayed. It means that the people of God who trust in him shall become strong in faith; able to contend with their spiritual foes, to gain the victory over their sins, and to meet the trials of life. God gives them strength, if they seek him in the way of his appointment - a promise which has been verified in the experience of his people in every age.

They shall mount up with wings as eagles. They shall put forth fresh feathers like the mounting eagle. It has been a common and popular opinion that the eagle lives and retains his vigor to a great age; and that, beyond the common lot of other birds, he pedestals in his old age.

He is teaching you to war with your hands; to remain steadfast in His love for you; to know who you are and who your enemy is. While you pray and wait on God, He is actively working on your behalf in ways you cannot see! God is working on your character to conform to Christ likeness. Jealousy, anger, bitterness, lust, and more are killers of a God ordained plan! He wants you to get rid of these so you can experience all He has for you! So that, when the vision is fulfilled, your character will prepare you to be ready.

Your experiences don't come to break you; and God does not send them to teach you a lesson. Life itself, in a fallen world, with fallen people will automatically teach you lessons. God will take these opportunities to make you stronger in the adversities; conquering and triumphing over them! Lastly, God's timing is not ours. The enemy will hinder you away from the plan of God. You and other people involved have to cooperate with God.

Another case scenario, a person praying to get a beautiful new home; they have done all their homework; credit is good, paying bills on time, has savings for down payment, and are financially stable. They are believing God and it looks like they will get this beautiful home that they fell in love with! The current owner of the home they are set to purchase, suddenly changes their minds during closing, and will not sell. You are disappointed! God will not come against that owner's free will. He may through another interested participant or the owner's themselves; move on their heart to reconsider. But if they do not agree; God is not controlling that person. You will get another opportunity for a beautiful home! This one was not for you at least not now. Maybe there is the right one, a couple of searches ahead! God is not into coveting also; you need to move on about it. If it comes back around at another opportune time, great, go for it. But all parties involved will have agreed now. I believe, God will, work it out if seems good to Him and His will. The parties involved have to line up with the will of God for the individual praying. He will not make something happen just because you wish it.

I've heard of so many testimonies where someone was waiting for a mate, a marriage partner, and they believed God had a certain person in mind. The object of your affections was not privy to the conversation between you and God and so, did not agree with your assessment. They did not hear God as you say and are not convicted or at peace about it. But if God really said it, He would bring it to pass in another season, in His own way, at another time. The other person will then know it too. If not, and in either case, you need to move on. The other person through their free will, later cooperates with God and will see this one is the right one for them. Therefore, whom God has joined together let no man put asunder. Time was needed for all parties involved to hear from God! The opposite can be true, of course, where a person heard wrongly this person was for them. God did not say it, or the other person did not agree with it. Whatever the situation for you, it is a waiting time before when you ask and when you receive. In many cases, God is working on you to see the answer.

According to the Bible, God works in seasons! Those seasons, it is possible to see the timing of God at work! For example, we know from the word of God, the sun and moon were created to help us know one day from another and the different seasons of the year. The climate is an indicator of winter, spring, summer, and autumn. God also put laws in the earth, using the comparison of the farmer sowing the seed.

Genesis 8:22 NKJV, "While the earth remains, seed time and harvest, cold and heat, winter and summer and day and night shall not cease."

Ecclesiastes 3:1, "To everything there is a season,
A time for every purpose under heaven."

Season is a period of time; to make competent through trial and experience. Purpose means a desired or intended result or effect. The farmer sows the seed in the ground, plowing, watering, tending, and pruning. Day and night come and then one day the harvest sprouts up! How does this happen, with a seed. There is a time to plant the seed and a time to gather. Understanding this principle, will help you to wait more patiently, trusting the Lord and being confident, God is working behind the scenes for your good and His glory!

Time and seasons are instruments of measurement, assessment, planning and perfection. Time is an effective tool in the hands of God in planning and executing his plans on the earth. In time, everything that has a beginning must have an end. If God did not create time and seasons, there will be no end to terror, sickness, disease, misfortune, misunderstanding, quarrels, poverty and illiteracy, failure and disappointment, corruption, and wickedness. In fact, there will be no end to evil.

While you are waiting, the Bible tells us to be busy about the Father's business. What is His business? God is in the soul winning and blessing other's company of which you are a partner! Serving others and being a blessing to someone else takes your mind off yourself. Thinking of the needs of another helps you not to waste time but be productive and accomplish many goals. It's not that God is so busy Himself and is consumed with billions of people on the globe. No, on the contrary, He is God and can handle all your needs, problems, and everyone else at the same time. After all, He created the heavens and the earth without our help!

In your waiting for the promise to manifest, no matter how long, you can become rooted in your position in Christ and live in that victory, stand in the victory that is yours. Being confident of who God is and knowing He is for you! Sure, of His love for you and the plan He has for the Believer and in your life! For example, in the world today, many people are fearing the coronavirus. Some think God has sent a plague to punish us and some believe this will never end. Thousands have reportedly died, and churches and schools where shut down for months. The world may be shaken but, we can choose not to fear and allow peace to fill our hearts, trusting God and His plan for the Believer. We can know this plan by reading and studying the Bible. God has said He is not sending viruses to us because of the Cross of His Son, Jesus Christ! He has made a covenant with Jesus, for us, withholding His judgment until that Day!

Isaiah 54:15 NKJV, "Indeed they shall surely assemble, but not because of Me. Whoever assembles against you shall fall for your sake. No weapon formed against you shall prosper. And every tongue which rises against you in judgment you shall condemn. This is the heritage of the servants of the Lord and their righteousness is from Me says the Lord."

Things to remember; we do have an enemy; we live in a fallen world (this is not the world God created for us) and we all have free wills (which are subject to error). The enemy is at work in the world but know for sure, man is also capable of destroying themselves. God gives us control over the earth. But because of His goodness, and through prayer, His angels are sent to aid us. Some of the covenant promises of being a child of God! He has not left us helpless!

We have assuredly, the Holy Spirit in the earth, and dwelling in every Believer, to lead, guide, comfort and encourage us in this life! God has well equipped the Believer and empowered us with His Spirit and Nature! The book of Ephesians tells us to put on the full armor of God, weapons for battle! God says to put it on every day! This armor is: truth, righteousness, gospel of peace, faith, salvation, the word of God and prayer!

Isaiah 30:21 NKJV, "Your ears shall hear a word behind you saying, this is the way, walk in it. Whenever you turn to the right hand or whenever you turn to the left."

You cannot know the plan of God for your life without much prayer! Prayer is paramount while you are waiting on the Lord. Before your prayer is answered, you need to seek God for instruction. When you hear the instruction, you need to act. Doing so, is stating you have faith in what you heard and moving in that direction is your act of faith. Faith without works or actions is dead. Meaning your faith is lifeless and will produce no fruit in your life. As you move in the direction you believe you heard God, you are acting in faith. God sees this and He knows you do not know everything. He just wants you to trust Him and rely in His ability to lead you!

Proverbs 3:5, 6 AMPC, "Lean on, trust in, and be confident in the Lord with all your heart and mind and do not rely on your own insight or understanding. In all your ways know, recognize, and acknowledge Him and He will direct and make straight and plain your paths."

It is difficult for people to believe in something we do not see and to follow someone we do not understand, because we like knowing what is in front of us. Faith takes us out of our comfort zone and brings us into the unknown. A lot of people do not like surprises and want to know what is going on all the times, but some of this can be fear and trust issues.

In order to advance to the next level of wherever you are in your walk with God, you will go through countless times of change. Change directions, actions of faith are required and necessary for your growth in knowing and trusting God! You need prayer and listening skills coupled with patience to know what God is saying and being obedient to act on His instructions. Depending on how this is implemented in your personal life, could delay, or positively could cause you to reach your destination without much stress.

When I first starting discerning the voice of God and His ways, it startled me and was exciting at the same time. The more time I spent with Him, the more faith developed in me, trusting Him. If you really trust someone, you will follow them anywhere they lead! Through many challenges where it seems you've hit rock bottom and when many things in your life appears to be not succeeding, you can still learn to trust God. Purpose to discipline yourself and be open to learning and applying the word of God!

Being confident of this thing, God is presently actively working on your behalf! Although, God is not in a hurry; we are the ones who are impatient, be encouraged! Know that in His timing, He will work all things out for your good, if you just wait!

Chapter 5

Discern & Hear God's Voice

Some say, they have not heard God speak in an audible voice, but how many cannot hear Him because it does not sound like we want Him to? Hearing God for a Believer should be as normal as speaking to another. For the average Christian, it has been one of the most difficult. You cannot have an intimate relationship with God without knowing His voice! Whether it sounds audible to you or not, you will need to be at least familiar with what He sounds like.

Jesus the Good Shepherd:

John 10: 3-5 CSB, "The gatekeeper opens the gate for him, and the sheep listen to his voice. He calls his own sheep by name and leads them out. [4] When he has brought out all his own, he goes on ahead of them, and his sheep follow him because they know his voice. [5] But they will never follow a stranger; in fact, they will run away from him because they do not recognize a stranger's voice."

The Lord God compares natural things to convey a spiritual truth so we can understand the lesson. Here Jesus is referred to as the Good Shepherd who is the caretaker of the sheep (Believers). He is not only the Shepherd but a Good Shepherd. Jesus is the Gatekeeper, an attendant at a gate controlling who goes through it. He is our provider and protector. The sheep are acquainted with the Shepherd and know His voice. The sheep follow the Shepherd and will not follow a stranger!

I'm not sure why there is a reluctance among the Believer's regarding hearing the audible voice of God. Why would this be surprising? Audible simply means clear, easy to hear, noticeable, or loud. The first time I heard the voice of God, it was definitely audible, and it frightened me. I guess all the years of asking God to speak to me, He decided to make it clear! Nevertheless, it was audible. This is my story and I'm sticking to it! It was the early morning hours and was so loud, awoke me out of my sleep. I quickly arose and turned every light on in my home. When I realized it was the voice of God, peace filled my heart! I was so very happy! I was not frightened at all the next time and it quickly became natural for me. But the first time, I got up quickly and fearing to run because I was not familiar with His voice. You cannot have an intimate meaningful relationship with God unless you learn to recognize His voice! However, this is for you!

In the same manner, in order to know the plan of God for your life, it is necessary to know what He is telling you to do! God is speaking to you in many different ways. If you are willing, God will teach you how to hear His voice and know His ways! He may choose to speak to you through His word (Bible), through music and lyrics to a song, directly to your heart or an impression, and even through other people. Through other people, if you cannot hear Him; He will answer you through ministry of someone else. The key to listening to other people, however, is to discern what they are sharing with you; whether it is truly from God, is so paramount! Not hearing God properly can cause you to miss the will of God completely, or on a large part, or it may take a long time for that door to open again. But God is faithful!

The more we listen to God's voice, the easier it is to recognize when He speaks to us! So many Believer's say they cannot hear God's voice. God's ways and thoughts are indeed so much higher than ours, but He is not trying to make it a mystery to hear Him! He wants you to hear Him! He wants to communicate with you! Particularly a Believer, because of the relationship and we can know this by so many scriptures in the Bible.

For example, the book of Genesis tells us, in the beginning, God walked with Adam in the cool of the day. There was communication between them and fellowship. Nothing was blocking access to God. It was not a strange thing for Adam and God to talk. It was normal for Adam to hear God's voice. Adam had not sinned, and man had not fallen. Even after Adam sinned, he and Eve could hear God clearly. So could their children. After man fell into sin, it became harder because of sin to access God and before Jesus was resurrected, hearing God was only through certain people (prophets and priests) at certain times. Only until God rose Jesus from the dead, and Jesus had ascended back to Heaven, Jesus sent the Holy Spirit to dwell in every born-again Believer at the same time (Day of Pentecost)! We have the greater one on the inside of us, again if you are a Believer! God has given every Believer, His Spirit, so we can communicate freely with Him! The Holy Spirit is the Spirit of God (God Himself), who helps us to hear more clearly what God is saying. We will talk more about the ministry of the Holy Spirit in the next chapter!

Let's look at some possible hindrances to your hearing God!

Hardened heart

Hebrews 3:7-8 NIV, "Today if you will hear his voice do not Harden your hearts."

A person who has a hardened heart has stopped having kind or friendly feelings for someone or caring about something. You can develop a noncaring attitude in your heart toward God himself or the things of God. A very nonchalant indifference to church or the Bible. This has to be developed through time; it doesn't happen overnight and must be maintained. Some people when they get saved are on fire for the Lord. They have newfound revelation and love for God. They have a zealousness for the work of God! After time, the flame begins to flicker. The book of *Revelations,* says, *"You have left your first love."* You have become weary and no longer care with the intensity you had before. Similar to a marriage; at first you commit your lives and then after a few years, you cannot remember why you married them!

A relationship with God or any relationship, takes work, effort, determination, and commitment. Your old testimonies of 10 years ago without recent or even current ones, will not sustain you. Will not keep the fire ignited! This would not work in a human relationship. Why would it with God? You may have heard some say, "Lord if you never do anything else for me, I will be satisfied!" Really? We are humans, and God knows not to put this to the test!

This scripture in Hebrews, share of the experiences God had with the children of Israel in the wilderness. Where He showed them His works and they tried His last nerves repeatedly. God said they always went astray in their *hearts*. Their behavior and attitudes were questionable and in error. Just like the children of Israel then, we cannot remember what the Lord has done for us in our lives. We thank God at the moment, but then after a time, blame Him or ask, "Where is God?" Again, we grumble and complain, as if God has done nothing for us. We are ungrateful.

If we do not work on it, our lives will or can resemble that of the children of Israel. Who did not care about God or what He offered and hence, missed the promises of God! There is no one to blame but ourselves.

Not willing to listen

God's voice for the most part sounds like yourself! Remember the episode on the Andy Griffith show where Barney played with checkers with himself. He even switched seats to represent the other player, which was again, himself! This is a set up where you will always win because you are player #1 and player #2! We can hold these conversations with God, where you control both players. I believe, in these cases, God may actually be silent, wondering, what are you doing? Lol! Why, because sometimes we don't like the solution God has. We believe ours is better than His! You're laughing but how many of you have done it?

We request something of God but don't wait for Him to give the answer or enough time to respond in His own way; we answer what we think is right or what we desire, out of our minds and say, "God told me."

> *2 Timothy 4:3,4 NIV, "For the time will come when people will not put up with sound doctrine. Instead, to suit their own desires, they will gather around them a great number of teachers to say what their itching ears want to hear. 4 They will turn their ears away from the truth and turn aside to myths."*

On occasions, we don't want to hear the truth! It doesn't fit in our little world's process of thinking. This can be the case in our church attendance or membership. Howbeit, let me throw in this,

I do believe God will direct you to more than one church to be a member in your lifetime but there are times when a person will go from one church to the next, because they cannot find exactly what they are looking for. Or should I say, what they want to hear! Have you done a self-examination to make sure perhaps you are not the problem? God will not send you to another church unless there is a purpose in His plan for you in doing so. If God sends you to another church, it is good to stay planted there until God releases you for whatever reasons. It is been my experience that God will move you forward to take you to another level according to your growth. For example, some churches are more passive than others. There are churches that are radical in worship or preaching. I've come to learn, churches have personalities, like cities or countries! You may need at a point in your life, a more laid-back church and then as your walk with God progresses, this same church may not be feeding you enough!

Be careful that the reason you are not willing to listen is because it does not suit your purposes. Being sensitive always to the leading of the Holy Spirit! A person unwilling is disobedient! The Bible calls it rebellion.

Unforgiveness

Then there is unforgiveness towards a person who did something wrong to you and you want God to punish them. You believe God should agree with what you had in mind. Unforgiveness will hinder the flow of blessing to you from God, and you cannot hear God's voice! It is like a clogged faucet, which would cause water to flow slowly or hardly at all. The water is available but cannot pass through. Can be layers of mineral deposits and sediment that flows in the water supply lines until it lodges there, gets stuck. Layers take time to form and so does unforgiveness in the heart but once it is there, it sticks for a while unless you take steps to move it out of the way, *Mark 11:22-2.* The Father can't forgive us if we don't forgive other people.

Many people ruin their health and their lives by taking the position of bitterness, resentment and unforgiveness. It's burdensome to have hateful thoughts toward another person rolling around inside your head. It's like heavy bricks weighing down on you! Unforgiveness hurts you more than the other person. It can seem so unfair for them to receive forgiveness, but it will set you free if you can let it go and set the other person free too!

I too have had times of unforgiveness for a wrong done to me. Sometimes the wrong is perceived but not reality. Putting this in the hand of God to work in your life and that person, is an act of obedience. When you do, it feels like the weight has been lifted. God wants to help you both, but you have to let Him in the situation. When you don't, it feels like an albatross or ball of chain attached to your leg going wherever you go!

1 Peter 5:7 NKJV, "Casting all your care upon Him, for He cares for you."

Again, your fellowship with God flows freely when you're willing to forgive, but it gets blocked by unforgiveness. Forgiveness also keeps Satan from getting an advantage over you. The Bible says don't give the devil any open door in your life.

Decide to forgive, resist the enemy, and allow the Holy Spirit to help you! You cannot do it by yourself. Then pray for your enemies. God will surely bring deliverance to you and them and you will hear Him more clearly!

Traditions and religions

Mark 7:13 NKJV, "Making the word of God of no effect through your tradition which you have handed down."

Your tradition or what you are accustomed to will cause your heart to be desensitized to the voice of God! When what God tells you, goes against what you have been taught or believe. Or when what God tells you, puts conflict between myself and people I love. Also, when what God tells you, proves you to be in error. Sometimes, we just don't want to repent! We are enjoying what we are doing and know it is wrong. But we pray anyway and try to fit God into our reality and say He said it. If our way of thinking, does not line up or fit what God says in His word, it is not God's voice. Pride is dangerous because you can place yourself higher than God and become exalted in your own mind. This is what happened to satan. Measuring what God says in His word will lead you into knowing if you heard from God or not! The word says, faith comes by hearing and hearing by the word of God!

For example, some religions do not have a personal relationship with the Lord Jesus, but God has come to dwell in every Believer! There is no middle person; no organization that speaks for you and no man who is a priest. The word of God tells us Jesus is our High Priest and all can come boldly to the throne of grace, *Hebrews, Chapters 7, 8.* You cannot measure the word of God, that lives forever to a man-made tradition! There is no balance!

Vain philosophy

The Bible speaks of having a vain philosophy. This is where you have formed thought processes through your parents, school teachers, even political leaders, shaping your worldview. If this view, does not line up with the word of God or trying to fit your view into God's word; you stay with your views. Instead of renewing your mind to what God infallible word says! It is vain; producing no result; useless.

Jesus + another god

Jesus plus is for those who claim to know and walk with God and Jesus but have other idols. It is Jesus plus something else or someone not Jesus only! I once talked with a woman who was selling her home, she was a church goer, but the woman shared she got her house sold within a few days due to a statue she used for good luck. I was flabbergasted! This is Jesus plus something else. No, it should be and has to be Jesus alone! God Himself, says there is no other god, I know not of any.

Isaiah 44:6 NKJV, "Thus says the Lord, the King of Israel and his Redeemer, the Lord of hosts: I am the first and I am the last, besides me there is no God! And who can proclaim as I do? Then let him declare it and set it in order for me.

44:8, You are my witnesses. Is there a God besides me? Indeed, there is no other Rock. I know not of one."

As I stated earlier, you can know the voice of God by spending time with Him and hearing the different ways, He speaks. Discerning Him and knowing the character of God or His Nature. Meaning how God thinks, His feeling or how He will respond in a situation. For example, if you know God's nature is kind and has no characteristics of being evil; you can know He hates evil! Also, the way He responded to evil in the Bible, tells you God's ways. You may not hear an audible voice, but you can know what He will answer in prayer, based on his character. On the other hand, if you are not relying on His nature detailed in examples in the Bible, you will pray amiss and not receive the answers you are believing to. You asked outside of God's will! A person cannot know the will of God, the mind of God or the ways of God, without getting to know Him. To get to know God is through His word, by studying the Bible!

Not enough faith

Yet another hindrance of not hearing God is lack of faith or unbelief. Cannot have faith for someone you don't know or are at least acquainted with. The more you know and believe about God, the more trust there will be for Him.

Altars were built in the Bible, such as Abraham, instructed by God for a sacrifice. Altars were also built in the Bible as a memorial, to trigger your memory. Although, we are not instructed to build sacrificial altars today, it is beneficial to often remember what the Lord has done for us in the past! These altars build upon each other as stones to add to your memory book; a way of encouraging and reminding you, how God is faithful, how God is good! So when, the next opportunity arises of difficulty or a means to fear; we can have confidence!

A clear way to hear God's voice is through the Baptism of the

Holy Spirit! This is a gift from God to help you communicate with Him. More on this towards the end of the book!

You have to be opened to the things of God! To have faith in God, to know God and know He will reward or bless you for trusting Him! Many people miss the blessings of God due also to fear. Fear of the unknown and not understanding nor trusting God to know if He asks you to do something, where He is trying to bring a blessing in your life! But we won't let go, for fear! Abraham in the Bible is a fine example:

Genesis 12:1, 2 NKJV, "Now the Lord had said to Abram:
Get out of your country, from your family, and from your father's house,
To a land that I will show you. I will make
you a great nation; I will bless you
And make your name great; And you shall be a blessing."

The Bible tells of a man named Abraham whom God told to leave his family, friends and country to a place God chose for him. God wanted to bless Abraham! Abraham's father, Terah, was an idolater, a worshipper of a false god. God wanted Abraham away from his family for a purpose, which was to bless him and make him a channel to be a blessing. God wanted to be Abraham's God; to teach Him and do good to Him! God wants to enrich our lives so that we may be blessed and become a channel of blessings to others.

Hearing God requires a lifestyle change; a heart upward to God and surrendered. It takes times, patience, and an openness for all things new!

Colossians 3:15 NKJV, "And let the peace of God rule in your hearts."

Your **gut instinct**, or intuition, is your immediate understanding of something; there's no need to think it over or get another opinion—you just know. Your intuition arises as a feeling within your spirit. There is no explanation but are sure of something not tangible. Allowing the peace of God to rule in your hearts is even more than your gut instinct. Your gut instinct relies on yourself but your inner knowing (know that you know) relies on your experience with God and the word of God!

First, what does the word say about your dilemma? There are answers to every situation in the world found in the God's word! This will help you to make the proper decision and wise choices. God will back you when you decide like this. **Second**, ask yourself, do I have peace about this? There will be times, however, when you will not have peace and the word of God does not state in detail what you should do, but you have to decide quick? For example, when I was about to graduate from High School, I had been accepted to 3 colleges. Needing to decide so that I could accept one of the letters offered, I was praying about it. God gave me the peace about one of them. I realized years later, when ministry began in that same city, God had helped me to decide. There was no Bible verse for the names of the schools. I made the call based on the peace I received from praying! You can't go wrong having faith in God! God honors your faith! However, God's voice sounds to you, He will never say anything that contradicts His word!

Romans 14:23 ASV, "Whatsoever is not of faith is sin."

Chapter 6

The Holy Spirit

Much of modern-day Christianity sees the born-again experience as all there is to salvation. However, after receiving Jesus Christ as your personal Lord and Savior, the ministry of the Holy Spirit begins to work more in your life! The Spirit of the Living God is a person; the third Person of the Trinity, God the Father, God the Son and God the Holy Spirit. Three Persons, One God!

Jesus explained who the Holy Spirit is in the book of John. Jesus said, the Holy Spirit is the Spirit of Truth and those who believe will know Him because He dwells in every Believer and will be with them! Before Jesus went back to heaven, He said to His disciples, He would not leave them as orphans but will send another Helper, abiding with them forever! That is such good news! Jesus calls the Holy Spirit a Helper. He is here to help or assist us not to afflict or harm us!

Jesus compared the Holy Spirit to the Helper and the Comforter! Another Comforter; another meaning, one kind, just like Jesus! Jesus was saying, it is more to everyone's advantage for Him to go and to send the Holy Spirit! On the night before Jesus' crucifixion, Jesus said this:

John 16:7 NKJV, "Nevertheless I tell you the truth; It is expedient for you that I go away: for if I go not away, the Comforter will not come unto you; but if I depart, I will send him unto you."

Jesus said to His disciples, it was better if He left them, so that the Holy Spirit could come. Jesus walked with them and went about ministering but Jesus was not everywhere at the same time. He is God but, in some instances such as this one, He yielded Himself to be as man to help mankind! Jesus limited Himself in His body and to the Cross to defeat satan for us! He did not need to defeat the enemy for Himself; for He is God, but for mankind who needed saving!

What could be better than to have Jesus physically present with us? Jesus was saying, it is better so the Holy Spirit could dwell in every Believer, everywhere, at the same time! The Holy Spirit would not be limited to one person as He was, in the Old Testament before Christ's Cross.

The Holy Spirit was a necessary part of the Creation of the heavens and the earth! In the beginning, God created all the elements needed for His creation. Then, everything else was formed from what had already been created. All the essential ingredients were in place. But nothing happened without the Spirit of God. The Holy Spirit of God (the Holy Spirit) moved upon the face of the waters.

Genesis 1:1-2 NKJV, "In the beginning God created the heaven and the earth. And the earth was without form, and void; and darkness was upon the face of the deep. And the Spirit of God moved upon the face of the waters."

For this scripture, picture a drone lingering over an area in the sky. Watching and observing. The Holy Spirit hovered or lingered over the creation of God just waiting to bring forth whatever the Word said. When the Lord (Word) said, "Let there be light" (Gen. 1:3), then the power of the Holy Spirit brought that light into being. Likewise, with everything the Lord created and made, it was the power of the Holy Spirit that brought it all into existence. God the Father conceived it. Jesus spoke it. And the Holy Spirit was the power that performed it. Everything God did in His creation was accomplished through the power of the Holy Spirit. When God the Father was ready to bring Jesus into the earth, He took the spoken Word (Jesus), the Holy Spirit hovered over Mary (a virgin), and she conceived Jesus' physical body.

The Trinity: God the Father, God the Son, and God the Holy Spirit. They are One. In fact, they are so much one that they can't operate independent of each other. Jesus didn't do any miracles or start His public ministry until after He had been anointed with the Holy Spirit.

Matthew 3:16 NIV, "As soon as Jesus was baptized, he went up out of the water. At that moment heaven was opened, and he saw the Spirit of God descending like a dove and alighting on him. 17 And a voice from heaven said, "This is my Son, whom I love; with him I am well pleased."

What more does Jesus say about the Holy Spirit?

The ministry of the Holy Spirit began after Jesus ascended back to the Father in heaven. Jesus too had a ministry by coming to the earth, which centered around the redemption plan of God through the Cross. Jesus had to come in order for the Holy Spirit to have this ministry! Jesus Christ had to save mankind, in order for the Holy Spirit to be able to do His job!

We could not live victorious lives without Jesus and the Holy Spirit's ministry! Jesus made all blessings and promises available and now the Holy Spirit comes to dwell in every Believer, promising to never leave nor forsake us! Most Christians don't realize how important the Holy Spirit's ministry is or that there is one!

We could not know the plan of God for our lives without the help of the Holy Spirit. He helps us to walk in victory in this world and so much more! **You cannot discover and fulfil the plan of God in your life apart from the Holy Spirit!**

It is God who leads you in the paths you need to go by His Spirit. The Holy Spirit is a vital person in encouraging you along your journey. You will need encouragement, of course; as you inevitably make mistakes; sometimes others will fail you in comfort but not

God! He will always send someone, speak to your heart, a physical body to give you a hug, or through answered prayer, give you direction, and so many different ways to keep you pressing on! He knows the world we live in and the challenges we face! You may have a plan apart from God, but it will not be the best plan!

Jesus shared with us in how it was more advantageous for the Holy Spirit to ministry to be here in the earth!

<u>To teach us all things</u>

John 14:26, "But the helper, the Holy Spirit, whom the Father will send in My name, He will teach you all things, and bring to your remembrance all things that I said to you."

Jesus was about to leave the disciples whom He loved and walked with for years! He wanted them to know, He was not leaving them alone as orphans but would send someone like Himself. The Holy Spirit, who would be with them and in them forever!

The disciples could not understand what He was saying at the time, but they soon would remember and embrace the Holy Spirit! Jesus further tells them the Holy Spirit will be their great Teacher and teach them all things, and He would help them to remember all that He had taught them.

The ministry of the Holy Spirit is to teach, interpret, and explain all things He said to them. To make it plainer and more understandable; to instruct them in things pertaining to salvation. There has not been a day, that I don't rely on the Holy Spirit! In helping me remember where the verses of scripture are; in a better way to understand a verse of scripture.

For example, I could not understand, why God chose the nation of Israel for His chosen people, why them and not another group? I was curious and so I sought the Holy Spirit regarding it. My question persisted and I even asked others, but their answer did not satisfy me. It is okay to seek God about anything! One day, the Holy Spirit answered me very clearly. He said this, "I did not choose a nation, I chose a man named Abraham and made a covenant with him to bless him!" The nation of Israel came out of Abraham. God told me He chose a man and made a nation out of that man! Israel is blessed because of the covenant He made with Abraham! No one can teach you better than the Holy Spirit! There are great teachers of the word, but the Holy Spirit teaches us all! He knows all and can show you things you do not know nor can comprehend.

He'll show us things to come

Jeremiah 33:3 NKJV, "Call to Me and I will answer you and show you great and mighty things, fenced in and hidden, which you do not know (do not distinguish and recognize, have knowledge of and understand)."

One of the greatest invitations to prayer ever given to anyone was spoken to Jeremiah when he was in prison for preaching the truth. God mercifully spoke to him in his distress with an invitation to ask of Him and He promised to not only answer but more than he could ask!

God who is all-knowing, is able to reveal things that will happen to you. He knows your end from the beginning! He will not reveal anything that is unnecessary for your destiny but only those things that serves a purpose for the plans He has for your life. We are not able to handle knowing everything it would scare us or be overwhelming! God knows how to reveal over time.

Our Heavenly Father knows what you need before you ask, but it requires faith to ask. For when a person asks, they are expecting to receive from Him because they believe that He is able to supply. God wants you to seek Him because He wants to help you!

There are times, we don't ask God because although, we believe He is God and able, but we are really doubting is if He will do it for us!

Hebrews 11:6 NIV, "And without faith it is impossible to please God, because anyone who comes to him must believe that he exists and that he rewards those who earnestly seek him." ... Anyone who wants to come to him must believe that God exists and that he rewards those who sincerely seek him."

I've heard someone say that although, they were believing for a spouse, they would not ask God in prayer. Whether this person physically went on their knees or not, I cannot say, but I would guess because God looks at the heart, He already knew their silent verbal request. He gave them the desires of their heart! He wants you to believe not only He is able, but He will answer you!

He'll glorify Jesus

John 16: 13,14 NIV, "But when He, the Spirit of Truth, comes, He will guide you into all the truth. He will not speak on His own; He will speak only what He hears, and He will tell you what is yet to come. [14] He will glorify Mw because it is from Me that He will receive what He will make known to you."

The ministry of the Holy Spirit will guide you into all truth. As the Spirit reveals truth, He will always do that which glorifies Jesus! The desire of the Holy Spirit is to bring glory and honor, not to Himself, but to the Lord Jesus Christ. He testifies of Jesus!

The Bible tells us, the Spirit reveals the things freely given to us by God! Causing us to glorify the Lord Jesus!

Romans 8:32 NKJV, "He who did not spare His own Son, but delivered Him up for us all, how shall He not with Him also freely give us all things?"

Reprove the world of sin, righteousness and of Judgment

Part of the ministry of the Holy Spirit is to rebuke or admonish; to convict or convince; tell a fault to unbelievers, of their sin. What sin? Not believing on Jesus!

So right now, the Holy Spirit is not condemning in the sense of judgment but for you to realize God has dealt with your sin through the finished work of the Cross; so, you will be more willing to come to Jesus!

An animal is hesitant to come to you if it does not know you or vice versa. But once the confidence has been established, the person or animal comes closer! If you can realize, God is not angry with you, would you come closer to Him? Of course, most would! On the other hand, if you believe God is going to get you, you will shy away. This is what happened, again to Adam and Eve after they sinned. They hid themselves because they knew they had done wrong. We can relate to this with a parent to our children.

The ministry of the Holy Spirit helps you to realize your righteousness apart from God's, is filthy rags to Him! What do I mean by righteousness? Righteousness is one of the chief attributes of God as portrayed in the Bible. Its chief meaning concerns ethical conduct. Righteousness is defined as God's standards: way of doing things. That a Sinner turned Believer is declared righteous by God purely by God's grace through faith in Christ, and thus all depends on Christ's merit and worthiness, rather than on one's own merit and worthiness.

The Holy Spirit makes us aware that we have a Savior, Jesus Christ! So that we cannot try to justify ourselves. Of pending judgment; for not receiving Jesus! Because of the grace of God, we are in an era of grace. He was defeated at the cross but still roams about seeking who he may devour but one day, God will end this and the devil and all those who have rejected Jesus, the gift of God, will be punished. Because they did not accept the sacrifice (required by God) for sin through His Son, Jesus. After their death, the judgment will fall back on them in this case!

Our Comforter

2 Corinthians 1:3,4 NKJV, "Blessed be the God and Father of our Lord Jesus Christ, the Father of mercies and God of all comfort, who comforts us in all our tribulation, that we may be able to comfort those who are in any trouble, with the comfort with which we ourselves are comforted by God."

The Holy Spirit is our Comforter, who comforts us so that we may also comfort others in their time of need. He encourages us to keep pressing forward, trusting God and everything and every situation. The Holy Spirit ministering in this way is more greatly felt at a funeral, or nursing home or let's say a hospital! His ministry is deeply appreciated if you can discern Him, after a bad day. This is what He is here for!

There are times, when I've felt the Holy Spirit's presence; particularly when I am going through a heartache. It feels like a saturation or engulfing; in which I've come to know it is the Spirit of God comforting me or giving me a hug! It is very tangible and brings me much peace. I am able to be still and relax within moments! God who is All Knowing, will also comfort me before what could have been a crisis arises. When it happens, I am not as deeply affected because the Holy Spirit prepared me beforehand! There are other times, God will use a person who comes to speak words of encouragement and love to uplift your spirits. This is a vessel of God to flow through to reach you at that time! A smile on a passerby's face, a warm greeting, a compliment in the checkout line, all are ways the Spirit of the Living God will minister; encourage and exhort you to press on!

He instructs us which way to go

Isaiah 30:21 NKJV, "Your ears show hear a word behind you, saying, this is the way, walk in it, whenever you turn to the right hand or wherever you turn to the left."

Ministry of the Holy Spirit gives you direction! This can be achieved through a danger or warning alert up ahead or in the stillness of the night. In a dream or in a quiet moment of meditation reading the Bible! Recalling us when we go out of the way to change direction to where we ought to go. Letting us know we have made an error. The Holy Spirit is like the wind on a light breezy day gently in our ears, saying not that way but this. The Holy Spirit is not here to drill or admonish but to steer us in going the correct way!

To draw you to receive salvation

John 6:44 NKJV, ""No one can come to me unless the Father who sent me draws them, and I will raise them up at the last day."

A man is attracted by that which he delights in. Green foliage to a sheep, he is drawn by it: toys or candy to a child and is drawn by them. They run wherever the person runs who shows these things: they run after him, but they are not forced to follow; they run, through the desire they feel to get the things they delight in. So, God draws man by His Spirit. He shows him his wants - He shows the Savior, Jesus Christ whom he has provided for him. The man feels himself a lost sinner; and, through the desire which he finds to escape hell, and get to heaven, he comes unto Christ, that he may be justified by his blood. Unless God draws, no man will ever come to Christ; because none could, without this drawing, ever feel the need of a Savior.

It is the wonderful work of the Holy Spirit that lures or entices you as a sinner to receive eternal life. Because it is the best for you not to perish and God never intended for that nor created you with this in mind. God, our Creator, created you to live eternally with Him in perfect state of peace, joy and fellowship and all that it entails!

This was lost at the fall of mankind, but through Jesus Christ blood and sacrifice on the Cross, we have been restored back to God! This is an invitation by God, but it is your choice!

When a person receives Jesus, the Holy Spirit baptizes you into the Body of Christ and you become a body of Believers. The Holy Spirit is a witness with our spirits (we are spirit clothed in flesh); we are the sons of God!

The Baptism of the Holy Spirit

The new birth or being born again qualifies you to live victoriously on earth. Baptism in the Holy Spirit enables you to live it or to walk it out. We need the Holy Spirit; without Him, we would have no victory in this life. It is the ministry of the Holy Spirit, the indwelling of the nature of God to true Believers and the finished work of the Cross of Jesus that promises victory in our lives! The Holy Spirit assures us of final victory!! A home in heaven and eternal reign on a new earth!

Effective Witnesses

Acts 1:8 NKJV, "But you shall receive power, when the Holy Spirit has come upon you, and you shall be witnesses to Me in Jerusalem, and in all Judea and Samaria, and to the end of the earth."

You shall be witnesses - For this purpose we are appointed. We walk with God, commune with Him, read His word, spend time in prayer and devotionals and we share with others about Him. We are being prepared to be witnesses daily! The first Disciples were prepared and listened to His teachings and instructions for three years. They observed His manner of life, His miracles, His meekness, and His sufferings. They ate with Him as a friend. They saw Him risen and ascend back into heaven. We are qualified after spending time with Jesus to bear witness to Him in all parts of the earth. Wherever He sends us testifying of what we know of Him! We need the Holy Spirit's power! Jesus made it possible for eternal life! Jesus taught us how to obtain this eternal life. His teachings are in the Bible! The Holy Spirit keeps us saved and empowers us to live on the earth and anoints us for battle over the enemy.

The Holy Spirit reveals the Love of God!

Romans 5:5 NKJV, "Now hope does not disappoint, because the love of God has been poured out in our hearts by the Holy Spirit who was given to us."

We have a hope that God is for us revealed to us by the Holy Spirit in our hearts! We experience the love of God through the Holy Spirit. To pour out is to express freely or to send (a liquid, fluid) flowing or falling, as from one container to another. For example, to pour a glass of milk; to pour water on a plant. The Holy Spirit flows to our hearts expressing how deeply God loves us! Have you heard someone say, "I felt the love of God today?" We know how this feels by His Spirit (Holy Spirit)!

We can know how much God loves us by the word of God too! There is a song named, "Yes Jesus Loves Me." A lot of times, children are taught this, often in a church environment. The words to the song go on to say how you know Jesus loves you; the answer: for the Bible tells me so! You can choose to believe God's word that He loves you and died for you so that you may have eternal life. Simply because He told us.

John 3:16 NIV, "For God so loved (prized) the world, He gave His only begotten Son. That whomsoever believes in Him, shall not perish but have everlasting life."

If we cannot believe God loves us, it will be hard to believe the rest of the Bible! **For all the Bible centers on this; the love of God**! You may question, if God loves us, why this world is so messed up? I believe by now, after reading my book thus far, you will already know the answer. But I shall repeat; God did not create the world as we see it. This world is fallen, corrupt, immoral and against the things of God! This fallen world is an enemy of God! The word of God tells us in the beginning what God created for us and it was all "very good"! This perverse world is because of man's wrong choices to disobey God! The ministry and work of the Holy Spirit makes the love of God come alive in our hearts so that we can experience His love for us! God has done and is doing all He can, to prove His love for you!

Psalms 34:8 NIV, "Taste and see (experience) that the Lord is good."

Helps you not to sin.

Romans 6:17, 18 NKJV, "But God be thanked that though you were slaves of sin, yet you obeyed from the heart that form of doctrine to which you were delivered. 18 And having been set free from sin, you became slaves of righteousness."

The Holy Spirit, after your conversion, reminds you as much as needed, you don't have to sin. Because you have been delivered from it. When Jesus died for your sin (*in your place*), you also died with Him. When God rose Jesus from the dead, you arose with Him with victory over sin. We are no longer slaves to sin, as if we have to obey it. We have dominion over it through Jesus Christ our Lord!

Therefore, the ministry of the Holy Spirit is very important! He has promised to not abandon you, desert you nor quit on you! Allow Him to be your Help!

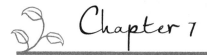

Chapter 7

Offenses Will Come, Even in the Church

A major stumbling-block the enemy uses for church goers is *offense*. Actually, being offended is a weapon against you in any situation. Being offended means to be hurt; wounded, resentful or annoyed, typically as a result of a perceived insult. An offended heart can stop or hinder the flow of blessings in your life from God. It is not God's will nor His plan for you, but some issues are blocking your way to receive His promised blessings in your life due to your being offended! As a matter of fact, it is God, who is fervently desiring and endeavoring to get you to see this; so, the hindrances can be removed.

Ecclesiastes 7:21, 22 NKJV, "Also do not take
to heart everything people say,
Lest you hear your servant cursing you.
22 *For many times, also, your own heart has known*
That even you have cursed others.."

Ecclesiastes was written by the wisest man who ever lived, Solomon! He was the wisest because God blessed him with wisdom. The Bible tells us to guard our hearts! Not everyone will understand your journey. That's fine. It's not their journey to make sense of. It's yours! Be careful who you allow to speak into your life. By the fruit of their lips you will know the roots of their hearts. I have learned you only get offended when you value what the other person says. Understanding this earlier in my life, would have saved me a lot of heartache.

When you value something, you consider it important and worthwhile. For example, if you value someone's opinion, you will ask that person's advice before making a big decision. Value has to do with how much something is worth, either in terms of cash or importance.

There is a balance here, that is often misunderstood. You can value someone as a human being but not to advise you or particularly help you make big decisions in your life. And certainly, not a stranger or someone you hardly know, unless God sends them; then it would require discernment. As a last result, God may only send them because you are not listening to Him. Or you cannot hear with clarity what He is saying!

Step back and see this from the other person's point of view. They do not know you, so how can they make proper balanced suggestions for you? For example, a controversial phrase in the Bible is "we are not to judge." People and most Christians take this to mean, we cannot have an opinion for it would be judging. The Bible does not tell us this, but rather "We will judge angels one day!" So, to say we are not to judge is an incorrect statement. When you take all the scriptures that refer to judging in context, the truth is we are not to judge to *condemn*. No one has the right to condemn someone else. Only God has that right! Furthermore, the Bible tells us to make a judgement conclusion, only when knowing the facts.

It becomes judgment when you say you know what is in a person's heart; why they said this and what their motives were. Condemning someone is to pass a sentence of damnation to eternal punishment in hell. God is the only one who can do this. He has given judgment to the Son!

If you are valuing or taking to heart what people say who do not know you nor the facts about your situation, how can they properly advise you on anything? Their opinion is just that, an opinion. Weigh what the person is saying to you in light of wisdom. Certainly, a stranger can speak words of life to you without knowing you but not everyone! It is up to you to decide whether to keep in your inbox or permanently delete it! If it comes in your spam or junk, be careful it may be just that or a virus to cause further damage. Again, if you believe it is something worth your time, continue reading after placing in your inbox. This will keep offense at a minimum!

We often separate ourselves from how we respond when we are in church and when we step out of the church doors. Wearing different hats. You carry yourself everywhere and when you enter a church building, you are not someone else (*I hope*). These principles of being true to yourself is to be applied in church, and in our daily lives. Whether on the job or traveling or at an event!

When a person begins their walk with Christ, it is easy to view another Believer as somewhat perfect, especially those holding leadership positions. If you are not careful, you will place that pastor or person on a pedestal of too high importance. Remember, they are to be respected but they are not God! The wrong approach is to forget that people are people. We all stand equally at the foot of the cross of Jesus. Everyone has challenges and it is not all about you!

I remember believing, in my early Christian walk, an individual who is born again longer than I in years, would be more mature. I've learned it is not the length of years, but quality of time invested in knowing God in relationship and His word. People are on different levels and walks of life. Extend grace and mercy as Christ has given us. Not everyone receives the same way or at the same pace. If we look at ourselves in the mirror and examine our motives more, our hearts would not be so easily offended.

Offense comes from feeling we have a right to be treated a certain way. We don't receive the treatment we think we deserve and thereby are slighted! Of course, no one wants to be treated unkindly, but it is healthier to try to accept case by case scenarios that everyone is not going to treat you fairly or the way you want. The world is full of relationships broken because of unreciprocated feelings! As Believers, we can mature in our knowledge and walk with the Lord Jesus, but everything is a process.

These unhealthy emotions come in so many shapes and colors! One year, I remember sacrificing a week's vacation to assist a friend having surgery. I was due only one week's vacation for that year and the surgery was in January! During this week, this friend offended me. Offense took the form of sacrificial help in using my only vacation for that year. As I was talking to God about it and complaining that I had every right to be upset after what I had sacrificed! God asked me to, "Give up my rights," I immediately understood Him to mean, consider not exercising the rights I thought I had and choosing to forgive my friend. After all, He had forgiven me of more this! He did not command me but lovingly asked me to think about my reasoning! The Holy Spirit helped me to see I was wrong, and it was not worth being upset over. As a result, the relationship continued on good ground; all went well! I took a step further to apologize for my attitude. My friend did not apologize; it is hard for some people to say, "I'm sorry," and admit they are wrong. It's okay for you to extend the olive branch! God was and is continuing to teach me to give up my rights when I get offended.

Offenses occur mostly as a result of a perceived wrong. Whether real or imagined, the person hurt most is you! You are the one feeling burdened, restless nights, and lack of peace. Could be, the other individual, either doesn't care enough or they sincerely don't realize they have hurt you. So, you're only hurting yourself when you allow this to ruin your day by causing you to lose your joy; it could cause sickness to occur in your body. It is proven, stress is the factor for so many illnesses!

It is wasted energy and you can lose hours of your time, even years by living in the past! These unresolved offenses will rob you of your joy and peace today and abort God's plan for your life. God does not want you to live a life of frustration and regret! He has a future planned for you. The blessings of the Lord make you rich in the things of God (peace, joy, prosperity), what your money cannot buy, and adds no sorrow with it!

Proverbs 17:22 NKJV, "A merry heart does good, like medicine,
But a broken spirit dries the bones."

A merry heart has no room for offense. The happier and fulfilled you are within yourself; the less negative emotions will take root. God is not unjust; He never tells us to do something without giving solutions on how to do this! It would be impossible for some and challenging for others to assemble furniture or equipment without a 'How to Manual.' God's instructions come with how to walk it out! He tells us what to think about, replacing the negative thinking with good thoughts.

Philippians 4:8 NKJV, "Brothers and sisters, whatever things are genuine, whatever things are virtuous, whatever things are good, whatever things are pure, whatever things are lovely, whatever things are of good report, if there is any benefit and if there is anything praiseworthy—meditate on these things."

Our thought life is the focal point of access the enemy uses to hinder us and thwart the plan of God in our lives! If we can, get our minds disciplined, half the battle is won! Believe me, I too am a work in progress! What you think about does matter. It has been proven, what you think, you become. You live out your most dominant thoughts. This is why God tells us we can control what we meditate on. The enemy will bring thoughts or images to you, but you don't have to allow them to park inside your brain. The Bible tells us to take those thoughts captive and to cast them away from our mind and only think on those that are good for us! How do we do this, we replace the negative with positive. That means that I have a chance to do something about **all thoughts** that are not well-pleasing to God before they enter my heart and become a part of me!

2 Corinthians 10:5 NKJV, "Casting down arguments and every high thing that exalts itself against the knowledge of God, bringing every thought into captivity to the obedience of Christ."

A good deal of the time, God uses people to bless people; This is why we need each other and why God says the second greatest commandment is about loving others and how you treat others. If the enemy can get you to be divisive to someone, you may miss a divine connection or key figure in God's plan for you. God can bring another way, but it may take a much longer time than what was intended. A trick of the enemy I have found is when God connects you to someone, the enemy will try to put division between you. To keep you from talking, hoping to delay or abort the plan.

The opportunities to be offended, will surely come but it is important how you respond to the offense! Whether your first reaction or delayed response. God never leaves us wondering what to do in any given situation there are answers in the word of God!

In Exodus 20: 1-17, we see the 'Ten Commandments.'
the **first four** Commandments pay attention to
how we are to relate to Him! Stating this:

"We will have no other gods before Him; not to carve images of Him or any likeness of anything in heaven or the earth; to not bow down to these images; not to take the name of the Lord your God in vain and to remember the Sabbath day for it is holy."

The **remaining six** Commandments state how we are to relate to people. How we are to treat one another! Clearly God sees after Him, how we treat each other is the most important!

Thereby, if we are offended at people all the time; we are not pleasing God and blocking the flow of our own blessings already paid for and available through Jesus!! If everybody received the blessings of God automatically; no one would be lacking in anything. On the contrary, there are a lot of struggling people because they are ignorant of what God has offered or do not know how to get them to work in their lives! The plan God has for you, will always include someone else! Your God-given purpose is not the absence of people; thereby, we have to learn to get along with others.

One day God explained to me, that we don't love ourselves, therefore, it is hard to love someone else. And we don't receive God's love for us. Once you understand just how much He loves you, it's not hard to love Him with all your heart, soul, and mind and to love others as yourself. Yet, many claims to love God and still don't walk in love toward others.

1 John 4:20 NKJV, "If someone says, "I love God," and hates his brother, he is a liar; for he who does not love his brother whom he has seen, how can he love God whom he has not seen?"

Absence of love is a byproduct of being offended. You don't love that person and see them as valuable. Envy and jealousy are emotions that arise from offense. Whatever the reason, whether your fault or the other persons, you can decide to not be offended at any point. In some instances, it might actually be God causing a relationship to break up. There are some relationships that God just doesn't want you to have. God loves the other person but perhaps has a different plan for them. He also doesn't want you to have relationships that might keep you from your destiny. However, this should not be misused as an excuse to end a relationship because you're unhappy.

An especially important lesson God shared with me many years ago; is that the church building is similar to a hospital, where care and treatment is provided for people who are injured or sick. The Believers are to go into the world and bring the sick or injured to the church so that we can treat or minister to them, in order for them to receive what they need from God! Keep in mind, however; the Believer are just vessels for God to flow through to the other person and even ourselves!

Mark 2:17 NKJV, "Jesus said, those who are well have no need of a physician, but those who are sick. I did not come to call the righteous, but sinners to repentance."

Here, Jesus is saying, we all actually need a savior, but some do not think they need Jesus because they are self-righteous. We are all sick and in need of a physician, who is Jesus Christ, the Great Physician and Healer! Seeing situations realistically, we all need saving from sin and the ramifications of sin. Jesus is the answer! It is healthier to see the other person as they really are, loved by God and just like you, needing our Creator! No one is better than the other and in God's eyes, He is no respecter of a person!

We are not to look to another individual to know everything, not a pastor, nor even the Pope. We all know in part. No one knows everything except God Himself! One day, for those who go to be with the Lord, will know all things but in this earth right now, we cannot know all. This is why we need God, Jesus, and the Holy Spirit to reveal things to us in everyday life and knowing the plan of God for us! We don't know what the next five minutes will hold or the next hour; certainly not another day. We rely on Him who knows the end from the beginning, not ourselves or others! When we have erroneous views of a person, we can easily form wrong opinions and make inaccurate judgments.

And everyone has a story, a root of what's happened in our lives. To see the other person with spiritual eyes, which is the view of God, is to have compassion. When Jesus was on the earth before He went to the cross, He healed all who came to Him in faith. But first the Bible tells us, Jesus was moved with compassion for the souls. They were like sheep without a shepherd. After the resurrection of Jesus, He is our Shepherd and we are His sheep.

Jesus paid not only all the wrong's we have done, but the wrong's done to us! You can be a Believer and regular church goer but not receive the blessing of God due to hurts and offenses in your heart toward yourself or someone else. It doesn't matter how long you have been going to church or born again. God is not holding anything back from you but your spiritual faucet if I may use for an example, is clogged up. There is too much dredge in your past. You can't go forward sometimes unless you clear this up! Often, the wounds run so deep; like feelings of betrayal, you can't get over it in your own strength. Surrender it to the Lord and allow Him to rid you of it!

There is another offense not directed towards another person but at God! Again, a perceived wrong you believe He has done to you.

Matthew 11:6 NKJV, "Blessed is he who is not offended because of Me."

Anyone mad or hating God does not know God nor His love! You have little understanding of what He has done for you! He loves you perfectly and has always given you everything He has! He gave Himself to die in your place. He bore your shame, guilt, and sin. Ridiculed and rejected by His creation! So that, you may have a chance to eternal life; knowing Him and His Son whom He sent for you! God made a perfect world for you. There was no sin, sickness, or death. These only came as a result of sin and the world became fallen and man fell! God is all about restoration and redeeming mankind back to Himself. But He will not force you. He chose to give you a free will; the ability to choose for yourself. He will not hold you captive or a prisoner. If you want to go from Him, He will let you but not without trying to chase you and letting you know how much He loves you.

It's not important what everyone says about you. It's what you say about Jesus that's important. Who is Jesus to you? Jesus is Lord!

Chapter 8

God is Your Source

John 15:5 NKJV, "I am the vine; you are the branches. If you remain in me and I in you, you will bear much fruit; apart from me you can do nothing."

Jesus is referred to the vine and His Disciples are the branches. This is a natural illustration of our relationship with the Lord. The relationship between vine branches and the vine. Away from the vine, the branches will lose the supply of life and get withered and then die. God is the vine grower. The image of a branch gaining all its sustenance and strength from the vine is a beautiful analogy of man's total dependence upon God.

There also is the "vine." The vine is the source of life for the branches. It provides the water and nutrients by which the grapes are produced. Without the vine, no fruit could ever result. Branches are completely dependent upon the vine. Without Christ, of course, there is no spiritual life or hope of eternal reward.

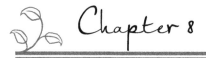

When Jesus Christ, the Son of God walked the earth, He demonstrated this truth, for He lived His entire life in utter dependence upon the Father. *I can do nothing of Myself,* He said, *I speak only that which I have seen from my Father.* Though Jesus Christ was fully God, He lived His life in His humanity. Jesus lived as God intended man to live - in total dependence upon God.

Our God is able to do exceedingly, abundantly and above all we ask, think, or imagine. Where God leads, He will provide! When God gives you a vision or plan for your life, He will give the provision necessary to fulfill it! He will not leave you in the middle of the vision. He is a Faithful God; this is His nature; His character and He cannot change who He is. People change but God is the same yesterday, today and forever. Unlike God, we are capable of gossip, lying, discord, revenge, or unfaithfulness. If someone hurts us, we are capable of unforgiveness and holding that person accountable. We are able at any time to wrongly accuse another. We are susceptible to rejecting someone based on the slander or opinion of another, but not God. God is incapable of denying Himself, who He is! He is dependable and reliable to not change His heart as we do!

1 Thessalonians 5:24 NIV, "The one who calls you is faithful, and he will do it."

When you understand that God is your supplier, and He gives you a vision or plan for your life, you can be confident He is able to make it happen! Your life's vision defines who you want to be, what you want to be known for and the set of experiences and accomplishments you aim for. Your vision helps define the goals by giving you a framework to evaluate those goals. Your vision becomes your why. This is why a company's purpose is called their **vision statement**. It is what the company is striving for, and what it wants to achieve. The organization develops a strategy to achieve that vision. Having a vision provides a sense of purpose and direction. So, it is with God and the vision He gives you for your life! Everything He purposes for you will center around this vision. Everything will be filtered to make the vision manifest.

God will give you a revelation of something He wants you to accomplish in your life that will bring Him glory! Something God sees you are perfect for and will bless you and others! The best vision is one that glorifies God and again, sees you flowing in your gifting! A person can have a vision that is now God inspired, but things will not flow well in the long range for you. Your God given vision will always evolve around the purpose originally intended, helping you define your short and long-term goals and guide the decisions you make along the way. Your vision will give you a conviction to always stick to the plan!

Generally speaking, a **source** is a place, a person, or thing from which something comes or can be obtained, like a birthplace or originator. A **source** is where someone or something came from. An example of a **source** is solar energy coming from the sun. An example of a **source** is the person who inspires you. An example of a **source** is the person who gives a juicy story to a magazine reporter. They want to know their history.

What does it mean to have God as your source? The plans you

come up with may work for a time but in the long range, they will not flow because you were meant for something designed only by your creator! And when God is your source, you can go back to Him for further instructions or direction because you will never know the full plan all at once and God knows the end! It is always evolving as God reveals more of the plan. Now, this can be exciting and amazing to watch and be a participant of God's plan for you to unfold or if you are not trusting and focused on God, you will most certainly become frustrated. This could cause you to give up and the plan be delayed, or you can get ahead of God and the plan be premature. It is best to try to remember, while you wait on God, He is working but you are doing something also; whatever He told you to do last until He gives further instruction!

I can remember when my husband and I were desiring to purchase our first house! We were living in a place we had not particularly cared for, but God had given my husband a plan! We took the necessary steps to pray and seek God where this house would be of course. Being fully convinced of the plan of God, we did everything in light of the revealed will of God. There were times because of our discomfort, I wanted to move prior to finding our house. But my husband helped me realize we need to stick to the plan. When God told us the vision of our first house, we drew the house we imagined on a large poster and colored it; then hung it on a wall.

Habakkuk 2:4, "Write the vision and make it plain on tables. That he may run who reads it."

The Bible tells us to write our vision down, so we may read it from time to time when the vision appears to be delayed. This will cause you to be encouraged and continue to be strong in waiting for the appointed time!

Anything that came to hit the plan was not allowed, my husband would say. We not only drew the vision, we stood on the word of God; writing scriptures down to remember. While you wait on the Lord, do something. Put action to your faith. Do something that is related in preparing for the vision you've been given. Such as, preparing yourselves for the house or business or ministry. Whatever it is God has told you, it could be a career move. Do your homework and get in position for when the door opens or God says it is time, you just walk in! There are some things only God can do but you can do what you're able to do. Not to help God out but planning to receive the blessings that are to come! I'm glad I listened to my husband!

In the Bible, when God used Moses to lead the children of Israel out of Egypt, His plan for them was to bring them *All* into the land of promise, flowing with milk and honey! A land of prosperity and He would be their God providing and protecting them from all other nations as long as they lived. He wanted to walk with them and bless them and show the world, **THESE ARE MY KIDS**.' God's heart from the children of Israel was only good. And this is the same way God feels about us today!

> *Jeremiah 29:11 NIV, "For I know the plans I have for you, declares the Lord, plans to prosper you and not to harm you, plans to give you hope and a future."*

God promised to conquer all their enemies. Every nation would fear God and Israel, fearing to come near them! When God led them out of bondage from the Egyptian's, He promised to take care of them in the wilderness and to see them to a land of plenty of food, nourishment, and freedom from slavery. God was the originator of the freedom. He gave them a vision through Moses of the plan. They only needed to follow His instructions. They were only supposed to walk through the wilderness in a matter of days. We see from their wilderness journey, many lessons! God shared these in the Bible for our understanding and so that we would not repeat the same mistake and miss the plan and blessings of God!

The children of Israel instead, like we do today, complain and murmur against God about what He had promised! Not seeing what God had already done. They were never satisfied and preferred the bondage to being free! Even though, they had cried out to God for centuries to deliver them. They trusted their slave masters more than the God who loved them! In short, they did not believe in Him!

Today, we want to know the plan of God for our lives, but do not want to wait on the Lord. It is hard for us at times, to receive delay's or the timing is not right; we want it now. We complain and murmur against God and it is just the grace of God and Jesus, He does not deal with us as He dealt with them in the wilderness. For almost all of them wandered in the wilderness for 40 years unnecessarily and there they died! God not counting them worthy to receive the promises!

The children of Israel also had more faith in themselves than in God. Time and time again, they saw His signs and wonders to provide and protect them. They believed for a short time and sang songs of praises but as soon as challenges came, they forgot the last blessing God performed for them! We do the same today. They did not see God as their supplier! That He started the plan by making a way of deliverance, going before them by leading them out to a place of refreshing from their scarred backs of lashes and harsh labor. But they complained they were going to die of starvation or lack of water. God's thoughts toward them were only good, but they always had evil in their hearts for Him. But still He loved them! When we get tired of waiting on God, we come up with our own plans, which displeases God. It is just His mercies because of His Son, Jesus, He is not angry with us today!

But the good news is, God is not angry with you because He sees Jesus as our Mediator between Him and man! There is a Judgment Day coming for all those who have rejected His Son but today, God is not even a little bit upset with you! Even if you have missed the plan of God or have not consulted Him about a plan, He heart is for you and wants to help you walk in your divine destiny.

Romans 8:28 NIV, "And we know that in all things God works for the good of those who love him, who have been called according to his purpose."

Believe me, you will make mistakes along the way, even after seeking God for His will and plans for your life. God looks at the heart, He is able to see your heart as sincerely trying. He is a good God and is so merciful towards us! God is cheering you on to the finish line, believing in you when you don't believe in yourself. He is able to connect you back in the right direction when you couldn't see clearly. Even in your disobedience, you took a detour, when He did not tell you to. If you trust Him, He will put you on the right path again! When you went too far and should have turned around, it may take a long time to get you to the place God wants you, but God can put you on the right road again heading in the right direction toward your destiny! But through patience and prayerfully seeking God for guidance, He can absolutely make it happen for you!

An issue of frustration for me was my dissatisfaction at seemingly temporary jobs. Through these, although, God taught me by His Spirit, jobs did not limit Him in my life. That He was and is my benefit! Most of us aspire to have a permanent job for many reasons not the least for the benefits packages; medical, dental or vision and more, which is nothing wrong with it. But the day the job lays you off, fires you or demotes you; your benefits gone. What will you do then? Who should you turn to? It is a mistake to put your trust in a company or business. No matter how successful! God was working in me His word that says, He daily loads me with benefits that far outweigh any earthly benefits. For He has promised me healing (mind, soul, and body), and that I will lack nothing to be victorious in the earth! Whether I have a job or unemployed, God will provide for me supernaturally! God resources are not depended on this world's limited economy or system (way of doing things) but on His unlimited power of supply!!

Philippians 4:19 NIV, "And my God will liberally supply (fill to the full) your every need according to His riches in glory in Christ Jesus."

Seeing God as your source, will help you develop confidence that He will definitely provide for you. People put their confidence in so many things, other people, jobs, businesses, or riches but these resources are bound to fail you at some point. When the economy faces failures, your business is forced shut, and your money is dwindling, who is your source. The world system will fail you; it is not loyal to you. Your business, however prosperous for you in the past, is subject to slip through your fingers. Your riches you put your trust in, is only temporary. One day you have it and tomorrow, you can be broke. Just like that!

Today, we are in a worldwide crisis that is unprecedented! The world is shaken, and people are much afraid. Things have never happened on this level. Some still refuse to put their trust in God, their Creator. Others are beginning to re-examine themselves in the light of their relationship with God and Jesus! The latter is most needful!

Mark 8:36 NKJV, "For what will it profit a man if he gains the whole world, and loses his own soul?"

At the end of your life, you cannot take your job, business, or riches with you! It is proven, some people who have these things, are not fulfilled in their lives. This is because these things are temporary and will one day cease to exist, but God is eternal! There is parable that teaches us we are to build on the sure foundation of Jesus Christ. It's a parable of two builders. One considered to be wise and the other, foolish.

Matthew 7:24-27 NIV, 24 "Therefore everyone who hears these words of mine and puts them into practice is like a wise man who built his house on the rock. 25 The rain came down, the streams rose, and the winds blew and beat against that house; yet it did not fall, because it had its foundation on the rock. 26 But everyone who hears these words of mine and does not put them into practice is like a foolish man who built his house on sand. 27 The rain came down, the streams rose, and the winds blew and beat against that house, and it fell with a great crash."

Putting God as your supplier, guarantees, when the famines

come, God will provide for you! God will arise over you and cause you to prosper. God created time for us, but God is outside of time. He is not limited by this world system. His resources are unlimited. His power knows no boundaries! You can tap into His resources and be abundantly provided for because He is your source!

In order for me to begin seeing God as a source in my life, required me to surrender in different areas. It did not happen all at once but as God revealed to me the errors, I was not trusting Him in, and asked me to give Him those areas to change my heart. Then, God replaced those things with Him being my provider. Such as my desire for family and lots of children. For whatever the reason(s), I have not had any biological children but once I surrendered that need, God has blessed me with many spiritual children. Through orphanages and the churches my husband and I oversee.

Another example of an area I surrendered is my wanting a husband. When I surrendered the need for a husband and totally relied on God as my source and husband (figurately), God introduced me to my husband on a mission's trip overseas!

God's plan for your life is ultimately a relationship and everything He plans for you is working in that plan. To restore you back to Him and be your Father! Everything He does in planning your life is out of His love for you! To bring you into the knowledge of Him and who you are to Him And while God is working His purposes in your life, He will give you the desires of your heart. True it is not all about you. It is about Jesus! But God is mindful of you and truly wants to bless you!

Chapter 9

Imagination Creates Reality

One of the greatest "tools" that God has given you for success is your imagination. When used properly, your imagination can become a powerful force for your future. Ultimately, what you imagine determines what you believe, and how you believe determines how you receive. Having a positive imagination is what the Bible calls hope! And hope is what faith is based upon.

Before God calls you to do anything, He sees you completing it! The word of God tells us, God created the heavens and the earth! That before He created anything, He saw it! He saw and then spoke into reality! Calling those things that are not into existence. Every Believer has the same God faith on the inside of you! Assuring us of what we can achieve if we can envision and embrace it!

Hebrews 11:1 NIV, "Now faith is confidence in what we hope for and assurance about what we do not see."

In the natural, we don't see it. Our minds aren't able to comprehend it fully! But since God said it, therefore you can see it happening and have confidence and be assured of its manifestation! We were created by God and He has given us the ability to create with our minds and with our words! We have power in our words! Your imagination can take you anywhere. Why not use your imagination for the glory of God!

Genesis 11:6 AMPC, "Nothing they have imagined they can do will be impossible for them."

God created us to be imaginative like Him! Men in Noah's time were imagining to build a tower to reach heaven. The Bible tells us they were going to use brick instead of stone, and tar for mortar. Because they believed without doubting what they imagined they could do, God had to block them by giving them different languages! "The Lord said, "If as one people speaking the same language, they have begun to do this, then nothing they plan to do will be impossible for them". Come, let us go down and confuse their language so they will not understand each other." So, the Lord scattered them from there over all the earth, and they stopped building the city. That is why it was called Babel—because there the Lord confused the language of the whole world. From there the Lord scattered them over the face of the whole earth. The people actually said "let us build *ourselves* (not for God) … and make a name for *ourselves* (again not for God, the Creator of all things)! God disciplined the people with different languages.

God knew with their imagination they may have done it, but this was rebellion. The people's purpose for building the tower to reach heaven was to make a name for themselves and not be scattered abroad over the face of the whole earth. God gets all the glory! God had told them they were to go out throughout the earth. God wanted to fill the earth!

Our minds and imagination are powerful given to us by God. But to be used for His glory and purposes! Like a loving Father, He will discipline us if we stray too far from Him! We are to use our imaginations in such a way to glorify God!

Pictures and Words

The imagination works even in a blind person because imagination starts in the mind! It sees beyond your natural eyesight and looks in the future. In other words, it is the faculty or action of forming new ideas, or images or concepts of external objects not present to the senses. While sitting in your living room, you can imagine yourself on a plane and taking a mission's trip or beach vacation. Imagination will take you there without ever leaving your home. A child can read a book about slaying the dragon and all its adventures; riding on its back; being in command; carrying a sword and going to faraway places with the dragon to defeat the enemy. All in the safety and comfort of their bedroom! This is imagination!

This was given to us by our Creator! Here is a point you know: when a child is being taught how to read, teachers or parents use books that associate pictures with words. Generally, photos of dogs, cats, horses, etc. It seems that our minds are designed to process images and pictures long before we can understand written words. This is why the word tells us to guard our hearts and be careful what you speak. Be mindful of what you think. Your heart and mind interact together. Should I say, your heart and imagination.

In the *'Parable of the Sower', Mark 4:1-20,* Jesus clearly teaches that our hearts are like gardens. Just as the soil in a garden has the power to germinate seeds, so your heart has creative power to "produce." Your heart tends to bring into reality whatever seed you plant in it. It has the ability to produce whatever is planted there.

Again, you have the ability to choose what seeds grows in your heart (garden). My husband and I like to watch Columbo! It amazes me how meticulously the criminal plots to commit the crime. The criminal plans day and night, how to accomplish their goals of getting rid of this person. They envision it from A to Z and they are consumed with every detail of the scheme. After they are sure of their schemes, take steps in that direction to fulfill it. They don't count the consequences just their wishes. These are bad seeds of course and planted in your heart will produce bad things. The point here is to use your imagination for the glory of God! Imagine taking that much time and energy envisioning what God has given you! This too, would be fulfilled!

Many people don't ascribe the source of the imagination, God! They think too highly of themselves, in their abilities and intelligence. A super business idea is one that someone imagines and has the courage to work about it. Verses someone else with no plan, who doesn't realize they have the same capabilities and opportunities to create, and lack's confidence.

A person, although afraid of heights, can imagine even while driving, leaping over mountains, or skydiving! Your imagination will take you anywhere you want to go. Of course, this can be in a positive or negative way.

Imagination has much to do with reality. It shapes the way we see our reality, and therefore, affects our expectations and hopes, our actions and behavior. Consequently, manifesting in your life what you imagined in your mind. God says it this way.

Matthew 9:29 GW, "What you have believed, will be done for you."

If you being afflicted, believe, and have confidence in your healing, being assured Jesus Christ paid for it at the Cross, you will receive healing! If you doubt it, you may not receive! God says whatever your faith is, good or bad, will manifest in your life! It's not God withholding, He is given you the ability and freedom to choose.

Deuteronomy 30:19 NKJV, "I call heaven and earth as witnesses today against you, that I have set before you, life and death, blessing and cursing; therefore, choose life, that both you and your descendants may live."

You can choose to believe and receive or doubt and do without!

The Bible makes it clear; God wants you to choose to believe and have the best He offers! He is not wanting you to fail but have the best life!

Genesis 15:5 NKJV, "Then He brought him outside and said, "Look now toward heaven, and count the stars if you are able to number them." And He said to him, "So shall your descendants be."

God told Abraham He was going to bless him with a child. Abraham and his wife were already old in years, past Sarah's child bearing years. Nevertheless, God said, he would have a son and through this son of promise, his descendants would be as many as the stars if he could count them. Abraham chose to believe God and here today, every person who becomes a Believer, is a seed of Abraham! Who can count all the Believer's from then until end of the age, but God! The word tells us God brought Abraham outside to look up at the sky and see (imagine) the stars. To count them but of course, Abraham couldn't possibly. He could only imagine! God is saying the same to us today, if we can see what He is telling us, and believe it, if will happen for us!

Imaginations are blueprints to a society! Roads, bridges, empires, and businesses are formed with the photocopy in your mind. A coffee shop, bakery, hardware store, apartment complex; SmartDraw also lets **you** insert your completed **blueprints** on an app or online. Get a plan and follow it through your vision; choose a location and one day what's on paper is visualized for everyone to see! What was in your mind and heart will become reality!

When we are told of how heaven looks in the Bible, we can imagine what the Bible is saying. Streets of gold, beautiful, no crying or sadness, no death and so much more. We can imagine all this and even we are going there after death if we receive Jesus as our personal savior, when as yet, we have never been. Our imaginations can easily take us there. It is a known fact; your life will go in the direction of your predominant thoughts. Again, your actions or behavior will follow your thoughts.

God tells us in His word, to take every thought captive to the obedience of Christ because strongholds form in your mind and can be a weapon against you! For this reason, the enemy wars with you to fill your thought life! Your battle starts in the mind because it is so powerful! If he can dominate your mind or thoughts, he can get you to act it out. Using our minds or thought life for good, will produce good things and we will act out what we believe or is in our thoughts. The enemy has to deceive you, reason with you in your mind first. You will act it out and the enemy just sits back and watches. He cannot make you do anything.

Since my early childhood, you have heard me say, I prayed for a godly mate of God's choosing! I desired to have the best person for me. Not wanting to be in a bad marriage because most of the people around me where unhappy in their marriage. Someone said to me, "You can be miserable all by yourself." This was such wisdom to me and so I prayed and sought the Lord for decades. Making a plethora of mistakes but one day, in God's timing, He connected me to my wonderful husband, and we are happy. He is God's best for me! I wish I had of waited with more patience and less complaining! As I envisioned what he would be like, God superseded my expectations! God is able to do exceedingly and abundantly more than you could ask or think.

Sometimes, waiting on the Lord can be hard because we are creatures who want everything microwavable, right now! You cannot have this with God, no matter how much you complain, blame, or explain. God knows what is best and the circumstances and people have to be ready. People have free will and God is not usurping that will He gave to them. It took time for Jesus to come through the wills and failures of men and be born a woman, it will take time for God to orchestrate His will for your life too.

A little at a time, God never goes from A to Z with us. Nor would a loving parent give their child too much too soon. A child doesn't learn to drive a car until it is a certain age and the maturity and other things are in place. It is understandable for God to care for us and not give us more than He sees we can handle. The provision will always make room for the vision. You don't need a million-dollar budget to sit on the couch and watch television or to witness to a few people here and there. If your vision requires a large budget, chances are you will need to have employees or volunteers, a building is involved with offices, traveling expenses and so forth. If you are in a place where God wants you, your provision is right where you are at the time. As the need arises, if you need more, God will supply.

It is easier to follow the plan God has for your life if you are doing something you love and have a passion for. If you are in a job where it is not what you are supposed to be doing or particularly enjoy, it will be hard to motivate yourself to even go to work. You are working in someone else's vision and maybe it's a vision you don't even agree with. You will not feel like you are fulfilling your purpose. This is because you are not. If you can see or imagine yourself doing exactly what God designed for you to do, walking it out, your reality will come to life!

Remember, endeavor to make the primary seed sown in your heart that of God's word. Let the Holy Spirit inspire you what to dream. He is here to lead and guide you the way you should go! Don't allow your imaginations to go unharnessed. Discern between good and bad. Follow the leading of the Holy Spirit with His goals, plans, dreams, and desires. It is possible to hinder or abort God's plan for you with the imaginations in your heart.

For example, a few years ago, God had shown me I would move across country to a particular Bible College. Never had I been this side of the country and for this long distance, particularly by myself. Not acquainted with flat lands such as the state of Kansas, I began to fear while on my journey. Prior to my departure, I watched the weather channel a lot and the news media, I've come to see are very negative and want to cause fear in people. What I watched a lot was tornado reports because they were a wonder to behold! While driving on my journey, I realized how frightened I was, looking on each side for what appeared to be a tornado forming somewhere in the distance. Howbeit, thank God, I made it safely but looking back, the overhyped weather reports produced or brought out my fears. The picture formed in my mind before I left, and fear grew in my heart.

As you read and study God's word, it will produce faith. The word of God is a living word. It reaches the heart and brings confidence and peace to your mind and soul. The more you read, the more faith will come alive in your heart! Faith will drive out fear or if you still have some fear, that fear will not overcome the confidence and trust you have in God! Allow the Holy Spirit to show you what is real and what is fake news!

Be sensitive to the move of the Holy Spirit and where He is leading you! Don't be afraid to dream with God! Take the limits off Him! Dream big! In order to dream big, you have to think big! How do you do this? By the renewing of your mind! Spiritually this is to change your thinking to God's way. Surrendering your plan to the Holy Spirit!

We've talked about it before, write the vision down. Make a drawing. Use photos to reinforce the dreams that God puts in your heart. Photos, posters, and paintings can inspire your heart with fresh vision and new possibilities. Realize that your imagination is like a movie "in process." Timing is critical. Wait for the vision. Wait on God's timing. Just because you see the vision, don't be anxious about it coming to reality. Let patience be at work in you. This will show your heart is to trust God and His plan for you!

Have you heard the quote, "If it ain't broke, don't fix it." Another saying is "We have always done it this way." Most of us live out of our memories rather than our imagination. We get stuck in the familiar and its comforts. The security of the familiar blocks us from moving forward. Your past could be unfulfilling, but we hold on to the memories keeping us using our imaginations. Thus, we are hindered from moving forward into what God has for us! This is what happened to the children of Israel in the Bible. God led them from bondage in Egypt, of mistreatment. They complained in the wilderness because of dissatisfaction and fear how it was better were they came from. But it wasn't a good memory for them. They could not imagine that God was taking them to a good place. They missed out on God's best!

Too often, people live off their memories. Allow God to give you a fresh word for today! God is into increasing us. Change is good and necessary, in many cases inevitable. For example, ten years ago, you opened a new business and today you are struggling. You have run the business the exact same way as before. Could it be, you have not changed with the times; creating more innovative ideas that has evolved with the culture? Even a house needs renovating; newer furniture and updated appliances from time to time. A website needs a new face lift to give it a fresh look. We live in an ever-changing world. Not all good but many things are, it is how you respond and view the situation.

The Holy Spirit is present and ever ready to help you with creative ideas how to prosper. He gives us the power to get wealth. The scriptures say, if you lack wisdom, just ask God and He will give it to you! God is the Creator of everything in the earth and heavens. He gave us our creative minds. Ask the Holy Spirit to give you creative ideas how to prosper!

Chapter 10

Social Distancing Not Normal

Genesis 2:18 NKJV, "And the Lord God said, it is not good that man should be alone."

According to the Bible, it is not the will of God for us to distance ourselves from one another! To be alone or by ourselves. Most of the time, the world is in opposition to God and the things of God. The enemy would love to separate people and get them alone to speak lies and cause deception. Teamwork and loving one another is the normal in the God's Kingdom! No man is an island to themselves. On the contrary, the Body of Christ is consisted of individual members who are not meant to be apart from the other; cannot exist or prosper without each other When one is weak, the other is to be strong for them! For this godly principle is for everyone, believer, or non-believer.

The human body responds to physical touches. Such as a hug, handshake, or a pat on the back. It is not normal, to want to be alone! In fact, it is so abnormal, people who are alone too much, feel isolated and it causes deep depression and too many times, suicide. This new normal concept is actually from satan. Remember, he has no new tricks but just uses different people through the ages.

The book of Genesis tells us in the Bible, satan waited for the opportunity where Eve was alone to speak lies to her. Satan was aware of what God had told Adam. There, he deceived Eve into thinking God was withholding something back from her. These are the obvious tricks of his even today! He is the father of lies, division and deception. He knows the strength we receive from one another and the effects of being in unity. Remember the men of the *Tower of Babel,* they were in unity in their thinking! Satan knows the power of the imagination and being one and single minded. For he himself, imagines he is greater than God the Father. God disciplined him long ago and his judgment is set! On the other hand, we know God commands us to love and help one another not to keep our distance. The Bible is full of these principles!

In the world today, we are experiencing an attack where it is causing most to fear being sociable unless in your own household. It has been called the, 'unknown enemy!' Let me encourage you, the enemy is not unknown, and Believers should not be ignorant of his devises, the Bible tells us we are victorious, and we win! When the enemy wants to bring destruction to your life, he first gets you alone to speak lies to you. If you are not fellowshipping with positive people or like minds of faith, you will be susceptible to the lies. For this reason and others, God has given gifts in the body to comfort, encourage, teach, and bless each other! He commands us to come together not run from each other.

Hebrews 10:25 NIV, "not giving up meeting together, as some are in the habit of doing, but encouraging one another—and all the more as you see the Day approaching."

Now this scripture is mainly referring to Believers, but our mission is to go out bringing those to the meetings. People of like faith in God and Jesus, need to come together. To be encouraged and give comfort to those hurting. You cannot know God's will for your life without involvement of other people, coming together to partake of the gifts in the body, to help you discover your gifting. God uses people to help people most of the time!

I Corinthians 12:4, 11 NKJV, "There are diversities of gifts, but the same Spirit. But one and the same Spirit works all these things, distributing to each one individually as He wills."

"Now there are distinctive varieties and distributions of endowments (gifts, extraordinary powers distinguishing certain Christians, due to the power of divine grace operating in their souls by the Holy Spirit) and they vary, but the [Holy] Spirit remains the same. All these [gifts, achievements, abilities] are inspired and brought to pass by one and the same [Holy] Spirit, who apportions to each person individually [exactly] as He chooses."

It is not enough to read the Bible on your own, but you need a teacher to expound on the meaning of the scriptures. Meeting together in a church or bible study group, gives you that help, so that you can understand the word better! Of course, the Holy Spirit of God, who lives in every Believer, is the ultimate teacher of our souls! In this type of setting, we discover our callings and giftings. Since God has placed the giftings in the Body as He chooses, it is an advantageous we come to the gatherings to receive. Of course, there are books or other social media on line these days, that will enhance your understanding, but it is nothing like being at a physical location of a local church! Now, obviously God is not limited just to church gatherings for you to know your gifting in life, but this was His idea. We know He knows what He is talking about.

As a member of a local church, is where God led me to discover my calling. There's encouragement for you to become more actively involved or participate in at least one ministry available in the church. personally, after praying about it and seeking God in what area, God directed me to the place I needed to be at the time. It turned out there was an announcement for a Missionary Teacher for children. Thinking back when I was a child, it was no coincidence, how I always loved to teach my dolls like they were in school. I would arrange them sitting around the chalkboard in my room, pretending they were in a classroom and teach them. Those desires were still inside of me placed there by God. He led me to a church that had the need for a missions teacher position at the time I needed!

Romans 11:29 NKJV, "For the gifts and calling of God are irrevocable."

You will discover your gifts or talents are already the things you like to do. If you don't have a heart for mission's, God will not send you to be a missionary. Or He will put that heart for missions in you! On the other hand, if you have a heart for mission's, it is God working in you that desire! Either way, you will love your calling because it is just you! I have heard there are some people, run from their calling, due to other's opinions or negative reports or even a selfish viewpoint of what they can do. But being involved in a local church among like-minded people of same faith, can help you to discover this. Not sitting at home alone or disconnected to others!

At a local church, there is normally a choir and praise and worship songs. There is hugs and handshakes, Greeters, or a welcoming committee. Some smiling faces. There is nothing like direct physical contact from another human being! We all go through challenges, good weeks we want to share, or bad days we want to cry on someone shoulder or just for them to listen. When we can go to a meeting and forget those troubles for a little while, be uplifted and receive encouragement to go on, makes all the difference. Many people live for this every week. No matter what is going on at home or in their lives, they can come to the church and receive the warmth and love from God and other people. Being welcomed instead of the rejection of the world and areas of your life, is needed so much in our lives!

Jeremiah 3:15 NKJV, "And I will give you [spiritual] shepherds according to My [own] heart, who will feed you with knowledge and understanding."

When we come together, we get taught the word of God in a deeper way than we can get reading the Bible on our own. Your pastor is not perfect, please give him grace! A good pastor plays an important role in the body and in the local church! He is there to be your spiritual leader and his wife if he is married. They are to lead you and help you discover your gifts and calling within the local church. And not only discover but walk your calling out in life. A good pastor, who is called by God, will feed you spiritual food (word of God) and sometimes natural! They will see to your wellbeing in every area. When the local church grows beyond his ability to help everyone individually, he will appoint other leaders to assist with the work of taking care of the members. Many churches have small groups located in member's home or Bible study groups, to care for those if the church is fairly large or growing.

You need a local church and you need a pastor. God will send you to the church according to your need and calling He has placed on your life. Your pastor should help you apply the teachings in the Bible to your everyday life. God uses nature many times to convey a spiritual truth or teach a moral lesson. For example, He uses the farmer sowing seed in the ground to help you see many things, such as, waiting on your harvest or breakthrough and giving. God knows we have to live in this fallen world for now. He sends pastors to help make the Bible relatable to you and your need. To aid you in finding scriptures to stand on in your situation at the time you need. If it is not practical, it is not spiritual. God is not trying to make it hard for you to understand Him and His ways. Your pastor should have a heart for people, one of love and compassion. God calls a pastor and sends them to the people. This pastor has the very heart of God and is continually seeking God to show him what is best for His people.

There were many times, my pastor taught on areas in my life that were relevant to me and needed adjusting. Obviously, I was not the only one in the congregation that needed to hear these teachings, for the pastor said the Lord was leading him to keep teaching on the same topic for months! Saying we were hard headed! Lol. Only God can totally give you special devotion and attention while giving the same to everyone else at the same time! God can do this for you, through coming together and the giftings in the body. Again, He can minister to you while you are at home, but there is something special when fellowshipping. Your pastor is hearing from God for you, on topics such as bitterness, loving one another unconditionally or forgiveness is helping you to receive your blessing if you can hear!

This is why I mentioned in a previous chapter, you have to guard your heart from being offended because these words can sting but if you can learn from them, you will grow and see more of the plan of God for your life being revealed.

Being connected to a local church and pastor who teaches the heart of God, will also keep you from making colossal mistakes. If you listen, however! Particularly when the pressure is on. For example, I recall a time when, I was really fed up with a job and was thinking of quitting. My pastor said this in a service at the exact time I needed to hear it, "He said he did not know why he was going this way in his message, but "someone is thinking about quitting your job and God has not told you to quit." He said further, "do you mean to tell me that you do not have enough God in you to turn that situation around? Take authority!" I do not know if this word was for anyone else, but I do know it was definitely for me!

The sermons were recorded but some editing goes on. If I had stayed home or not gotten the tape, I may have missed being comforted or could have quit. It was just a word from God for me at the right time! I reasserted myself and trusted God to turn the situation around and stayed until God released me. On that exact same job assignment, God shortly thereafter, had me start a weekly Bible study that lasted 6 years! Praise the Lord God! I would have missed the blessing to come, had I not been at church or heard God. Most often, God chooses to speak through other people, like your pastor. You are not the only one going through these challenges. The enemy wants you to think that you are. You miss so much by not being connected!

What about it, the enemy wants you to think by being disconnected, you have the worst possible scenario. You are a freak and even God is ashamed of you! If you listen, the enemy will have you believing things will not get better, just end it all! The enemy has no new tricks; he just uses the same one and speaks to different people with the same lies!

As I mentioned before, you will discover your gifting and the plan God has for your life many times in the regular local gathering. So, it has been for me, the connection of other people and not isolation have been most beneficial to me. I have seen others who do not stay connected with other Believers and they are just existing. We are made to not just exist but prosper!

Your local church probably has classes that help you to grow in knowledge and understanding of God and what He desires for your life, growing to your maximum potential and sowing seeds that will benefit others!

Sowing seeds or giving! When you are connected to a local church body, you should learn about giving so God can multiply the seeds you have sown and being a blessing to others.

Believers Are Salt and Light.

Matthew 5:13-16 NKJV, "You are the salt of the earth; but if the salt loses its flavor, how shall it be seasoned? It is then good for nothing but to be thrown out and trampled underfoot by men.

14 "You are the light of the world. A city that is set on a hill cannot be hidden. 15 Nor do they light a lamp and put it under a basket, but on a lampstand, and it gives light to all who are in the house. 16 Let your light so shine before men, that they may see your good works and glorify your Father in heaven."

Even in history, times of leprosy and bubonic plague, Jesus commands the church to be a light to the world! We cannot be a light with the doors shut. We cannot lay hands on the sick only via live stream. There is a reason we are to be physically present in cases of people suffering.

In the Old testament, social distancing ceremonies were performed from people who suffered leprosy. It was an incurable disease. It was feared that leprosy was highly contagious and becoming inflicted led to severe social stigma. In fact, those who fell victim to the disease had to cover their faces and yell "Unclean" as they walked the streets, ensuring that others could stay away. Also, in the Old testament, Elisha offered instructions to a man named Naaman who was stricken with leprosy. "Go and wash in the Jordan seven times," said Elisha, "and your flesh shall be restored, and you shall be clean." In other words, this was an ancient practice.

The church following Jesus example, touched the unclean with a heart of compassion. Jesus by laying hands on a leper, healed him! The church has in times past, even in danger, arose to be that physical touch of God's love to the person perhaps dying or receiving their healing! The servants of Jesus were brave and did not retreat. Some did but others chose to help.

When some cries are heard for suffering, we have brave men and women in the healthcare who tend to these souls. But the church is mute. These are difficult times for pastors. They are faced with decisions that has not presented themselves before. Howbeit, in a time the world needs the hope of the gospel, we must rise to the occasion.

> *James 2:15-17 NKJV, "If a brother or sister is naked and destitute of daily food, [16] and one of you says to them, "Depart in peace, be warmed and filled," but you do not give them the things which are needed for the body, what does it profit? [17] Thus also faith by itself, if it does not have works, is dead."*

Many are resisting to take risks. The attitude has become: "Go your way, be warm and be fed." The world is looking for answers and, the children of God should have those answers. We should not look like the world having the same questions. People want confident answers and certainty. The church is the ambassador for Christ in the world!

The world tells you what to do, mostly contrary to God; hide from each other in our homes. This is the world's approach and solution - fear, but it is not of God. Nowhere close what Jesus commanded us to do. The world has their own language, and this is normal to them. But should not be so for the Believers. The name *believer* means we *believe* in God! We must resist these changes as ungodly and be the hands and feet of God. Washing our hands with extreme care, will not wash away our sins and cleanse us. Only the shed blood of Jesus Christ has done this for all mankind! Prayers will deliver you from every evil work!

The church needs to be ready to give an answer in season and out!

Ephesians 6:19-20 NKJV, "Pray for me, that utterance may be given to me, that I may open my mouth boldly to make known the mystery of the gospel, [20] *for which I am an ambassador in chains; that in it I may speak boldly, as I ought to speak."*

Chapter 11

Time to Reevaluate Your Inner Circle

I Corinthians 15:33 NIV, "Do not be misled: "Bad company corrupts good character."

The kind of friends you associate with affects your relationship with God. People influence other people and depending on the relationship's you form in your life, will influence your decisions. Either leading you closer to God or away from Him. Your relationships with other's matter a great deal in whether or not God fulfils His will in your life!

It is important to understand that God the Father is no respecter of persons. What this means is that He has an equal and unconditional love for each person He has ever created, and He is not going to be playing favorites with anyone. Every single man and woman He have ever created is on an equal footing with Him. God will work with each person who will come to Him with the same amount of passion and to the same degree that He will work with anyone else. Therefore, there is an equal chance to enter into God's perfect plan and destiny for our lives - and then allow Him to build that life up and take it into the specific directions that He wills.

Even though, not everyone is receiving from God exactly the

same, He stands with open arms receiving ***All*** who come to Him in faith, through His Son Jesus Christ! Selecting or choosing carefully who you allow in your confidence, will affect your decisions you make with God. Give God chance to bring into your life godly purposeful relationships. Ones that enrich and bring out the good attributes God has invested in you! Your inner group of friends again, will cause you to struggle or prosper.

The people you befriend will greatly impact your life, whether for the good or bad. It has been proven repeatedly if you hang around troublemakers, you will become one. If you associate with those who obey the laws, it will help you to obey the laws. It is a mathematical certainty. God told the children of Israel to not mingle with other nations. Why, because He wanted them to learn from Him and not be polluted with ungodly ideas and lifestyles of other nations. He went as far as to tell the men not to marry those women, because they would turn them away from what God was trying to teach them. Some did not listen and just what God said would happen, did.

It is not God who is orchestrating and controlling your choices. He has given you the power to choose and make decisions for yourself. As for myself, God has sent mentors or advisors to counsel me in areas to help me make decisions that will follow His path for my life. He will do the same for you! I have heard many people in leadership say they are friendly with a lot of people but only allow a small selected number of individuals to be closer to them. Decide the friends, mentors & leaders you want in your life, in your inner circle. When you meet someone, always ask God to reveal their intentions & true character to you and pray for increased discernment. I can attest to being more trusting of people than I should. Praying for discernment will sharpen you in this area. According to how God answers your prayers of course, sometimes your circle will decrease in size but also increases in value. Don't worry about the number, it's the quality of friends you need and should want.

Surround yourself with those who will not compete but will sincerely celebrate in your success and see your accomplishments as a reflection of their own possibilities. Your inner circle of people should really know you and have permission to speak into your life. I always say with limitations. If they were to criticize, for example, let it be constructive criticism in a gentle sort of way. Not rude or demanding. There is a way to talk to everyone. With respect. If your inner circle includes friends, who want to always lord over you and never support you; it is time to reevaluate your choices.

We must renew our thinking in ways that are not pushing us to mature in the things of God. God will never tell you anything or remove anyone in your life that is not for your good and His purposes! God knows us and knows what is best for us, and if He says it needs to be thrown out or revised, it is to our advantage to pay attention! I have had lifelong friends, who God has separated from me. Some God prepared me prior and others, well, they just drifted away. This should not make you bitter or resentful. It may at first, but if those feelings persist, you may want to consider praying more for them and to God! To the best of my knowledge, these friends are born-again and that is the most important thing. They are not necessary to be in your life for various reasons at this time.

What should a circle of friends look like? Preferably, someone who gifted in the same calling you are, perhaps in a leadership position. For example, if you feel God has called you to open a chain of restaurants but do not even have one yet, someone who is already in the restaurant field or have restaurants they manage. This person can be a mentor to guide you in the steps to take. This person can be a teacher, a parent, sibling, pastor, or friend. They don't have to be in the same area of interest you have but as long as they add value and wisdom with care to your life!

Proverbs 4:23 AMPC, "Keep and guard your heart with all vigilance and above all that you guard, for out of it flow the springs of life."

An inner circle friend is not perfect, so please do not hold them to perfection but giving them grace particularly since they are closer to you! They may give wrong or bad advice, but you should know them well enough to discern if it is sincere advice! From their heart but having your best interest! Remember, it is up to you whether you accept or not. It should not break your relationship if you disagree and if it does, it is a revelation to you of that friendship.

A mistake I have made, far too often, is thinking that most

people I come in contact with are friends. Most people can appear friendly, especially at first, but that does not make them a friend. The old me, would call all my co-workers I sincerely conversed with, friends. God shared with me one day, because He kept seeing me get hurt by people, "Guard your heart!"

The heart is the man! The real you! God tells us He does not look at our appearance but at our heart! This is an astounding revelation! The world would definitely disagree with God! Vanity is the way of the world. The perfect figure, perfect hairstyle, perfect makeup; trendiest clothes! God says no, He is not concerned about this.

Isaiah 53:2 NKJV, "He has no form or comeliness; and when we see Him, there is no beauty that we should desire Him."

This is where the intent and motives are derived from! This is how He will judge us! To guard your heart is to set a strict guard upon our souls; keep our hearts from doing hurt and getting hurt. Because out of it are the issues of life. Above all, we should seek from the Lord Jesus to be enabled to put away a forward (willful and disobedient) mouth and perverse lips; our eyes will be turned from beholding vanity, looking straight forward, and walking by the rule of God's word, treading in the steps of our Lord. Simply to share, it is good to not be as open and naïve. You can be kind and still have discernment.

Do not seek to be understood by the world. You must look to an inner circle of people who really know you. Do not expect to have that kind of intimate relationship with people who do not know you.

Your inner circle should include someone who stretches you to take the limit's off God! Go beyond your comfort zone's level of thinking until it hurts! When you are working in a gym, sweating, and hurting, you know your muscles are being stretched. The aches and pains are proof of this. Ignorance is not bliss! God says my people are destroyed for lack of knowledge. They are His people, saved but bound in areas of their lives. Not living out the life God intended in this earth. They may arrive in heaven but limping and beat up by the enemy! There is no need for this.

Your network of friends aids you in reaching your maximum potential and you also should help them. A friend that challenges you to change your thinking process and you will change as a byproduct. God will send people to help you reach the place in your life you need to be. Those special gems! When someone is a gem to you, they are valued very highly to you. They stand out above the others. God knows where those kinds of people are and how to connect you to them! They will be a source of blessing to you in many ways!

This is an on-going process throughout your life. God will not send anyone in your life that makes Him unnecessary or the plan He has for your life. He will send people to lead you to Him. Whether encouraging you to read more of the Bible; pray more in the spirit, give more of your time or financial support, or whatever area you need to grow in. The more you know about God, it will affect how you relate to Him and to others. How you think about the world in general and your whole life will change for the better!

For example, if you believe you can lose your salvation every time you fail. You do not know the saving power of God! God is able to keep you until that Day! A person cannot lose salvation like you lose a hat or car keys, but you can reject God and walk away in your heart. But doing so, you will not be able to come back to Him again! Surely, this will affect how you relate to God and walk with Him. If you know, in your heart you are capable of rejecting God after receiving salvation, there is no chance of repentance, it will cause you to reconsider your ways. But at the same time, *"Isaiah 1:18 NKJV, Come now, and let us reason together, says the Lord"*, God calls us to reason with Him and search the scriptures. He wants you to make a good decision out of truth. Isn't it wonderful that the Creator of the universe calls us to reason with Him?

You need a friend who will encourage to expand your thinking. That not everything is always black and white but there are gray areas. A friend to awaken dreams in you left dormant by years of frustration or to even dream at all. To go read a book, use the dictionary, visit the library from time to time, take a class, or go back to school! To become a pilot, senator, or the president of the United States! That you can achieve anything God wants you to! Your inner circle should push you to go beyond the limitations in your mind!

Take the limits off God! God is not limited but you can limit God in your life! He will only move in the areas you give Him access. You can discover the plan God has for you and walk it out to be a blessing. It is up to you to make a positive difference in this world! Do not just coast through life, merely surviving but THRIVE!

Jesus Inner Circle

At some point there were 120 disciples who followed Jesus. Twelve were chosen by Jesus. These were His inner circle! He took very seriously the formation of this group of twelve apostles, praying an entire night beforehand. The twelve were closer to Him than the other disciples! It is worth mentioning that even in Jesus inner circle, these men were far from perfect. *One named Judas would betray Him,* the word of God tells us that he is a traitor who betrayed Jesus to His death. It is possible to choose someone as a close friend and confidant and they still betray you. This is a clear reminder that you never know the true condition of the hearts of people around you. The other disciples did not know this about Judas, but Jesus came to realize his betrayal. How Jesus responded is a lesson for us all.

Jesus loved Judas to the very end! God is wounded and humiliated by the betrayals of His people, but who nevertheless never stops loving them with eternity's love. Jesus humiliated by the treason of one of His closest companions, He kept on showing him his love. By lowering Himself before His disciples to wash their feet, He made Himself the servant of all, *Judas included.* And it was particularly with Judas that He shared a piece of bread. Jesus could have been resentful and hateful, as we all are capable of, but Jesus called Judas a friend! The night of His arrest, He kissed Judas.

Another disciple of Jesus inner circle was named *Thomas.* He was known as *Doubting* Thomas. *John 20:25 NIV, "So the other disciples told him, "We have seen the Lord! But he said to them, "Unless I see the nail marks in his hands and put my finger where the nails were, and put my hand into his side, I will not believe."* We often judge people by one mistake. We never let them forget it. Further, we never let the world forget it. In reality Thomas became a steadfast and loyal apostle. Thomas could not accept things without questioning them. He was a realist. Christ blames no one for wanting to be sure. Jesus did not condemn Thomas for his doubts. Jesus believed in Thomas and was patient with him. Answering his doubts until Thomas was reassured.

Your inner circle may include a friend who is like Thomas. But if God has laid this person on your heart to be included in your life, trust God! Your inner circle will include imperfect people and I hope they will have a heart for God! What you need to seek the Lord about is this person intended to be in God's purposes and plans for your life.

From the twelve, Jesus chose three to be even closer to Him, Peter, James, and John.

Jairus's daughter raised from the dead. There was a ruler of the synagogue's house whose daughter was sick. He came to Jesus to heal her. She died and Jesus rose her from the dead, *Mark 5:35-43*. The word of God says in verse 37, Jesus permitted no one to follow Him except Peter, James, and John the brother of James. The little girl was just gravely sick at first when the father came to Jesus for help! While the father was speaking, some came to tell the father his daughter had died. The Bible says, when Jesus heard the word that was spoken, He quickly assured the father, ***"Do not be afraid; only believe*!"** Why, because the father had enough faith to come to Jesus and faith is what's needed for God to move on your behalf. Jesus did not want the father to listen and be shaken to the negative words but continue to focus on his faith in God!

Furthermore, the Bible tells us in these verses, when Jesus arrived at the house of the dead girl, there was a lot of commotion. When Jesus asked them why they were weeping, for the girl is not dead but sleeping, they ridiculed Him, but He put them all out except the parents and the *three disciples*! Why, faith is the key and the single ingredient to activate the promises of God in your life!

Jesus was surrounded by faith filled people only in that house, in order to perform a miracle! In this atmosphere, Jesus rose the little girl from the dead! Praise the Lord God! Your inner circle needs to be people of faith in God! Let's look at another example of Jesus inner circle!

The Transfiguration, *Mark 9:1-13*. Jesus chose again, Peter,

James, and John the brother of James to take with Him on a high mountain alone to show Him His glory. They saw Elijah and Moses talking with Jesus. The word of God says, His clothes became shining, exceedingly white, like snow, such as no launderer on earth can whiten them. Here God the Father spoke saying, "This is My beloved Son. Hear Him!"

Again, for God's purposes and plans for your life, He will instruct you on who needs to be in your life. However, just before the *Transfiguration,* Peter had confessed his belief in Jesus as the Messiah and the Son of God, which the other apostles did not seem as certain or clear about. This caused Jesus to call Peter blessed, because Jesus said that this knowledge had not been revealed to Peter by human means, but by God the Father, and that it was upon this "rock" that Jesus said He would build His church. Peter became one of the most vocal of the apostles in evangelizing the people after Jesus ascension.

As brothers, James and John were close to each other, and also to Jesus, James would be the first apostle to be martyred for his faith. John later witnessed a vision of the events of the end times, as foretold in the book of Revelation.

It was Jesus knowledge of the faith and love of these individuals, as well as His foreknowledge of the coming events in which they would be involved to choose them in His inner circle.

The Garden of Gethsemane, *Matthew 26:36-46.* Yet another example. The night before Jesus was to face the most critical time in His existence, He came to a place called Gethsemane. Named this for a place of pressing or pressure. Oil press was a **garden** at the foot of the Mount of Olives in Jerusalem where, according to the four Gospels of the New Testament, Jesus underwent the agony in the **garden** and was arrested the night before his crucifixion. **Gethsemane** is **important** because it shows us another picture of how Christ shared in the human condition. He shared in all that we are including sadness, alienation, anguish, and death.

In this agonizing time for Jesus, He chose the three (*Peter, James, and John*) closest to Him again. Yes, in the beginning of the arrest of Jesus and the cross, all His disciples denied Him. Although, Jesus forgave them (except one was a devil), He still went alone to pray with *Peter, James, and John*!

We see in these examples of Christ choosing an inner circle, those who He relied on more than the others. Not all people and not all His chosen were qualified to go further or have deeper revelation of the things of God at that time, but He loved them all! Jesus only healed those who came to Him for healing and those who had faith, but He loved everyone! Jesus did not feed the whole world, but He had compassion on the multitude who followed Him. Again, showing His love for humanity and human suffering! Christ is our example. He loves every single person. This is why he died for us!

Love everyone, have many acquaintances, few friends and a carefully chosen inner circle!

Chapter 12

WE RISE by LIFTING Others

Matthew 28:18-20 NKJV, "And Jesus came and spoke to them saying, "All authority has been given to Me in heaven and on earth. Go therefore and make disciples of all nations, baptizing them in the name of the Father and of the Son and of the Holy Spirit. Teaching them to observe all things that I have commanded you; and lo, I am with you always, even to the end of the age."

Matthew 28:18-20 tells us that before Jesus ascended back to Heaven, He commanded His disciples (today every Believer is His disciple) to preach and teach the gospel, the Good News of His salvation and hope. Jesus commands us to witness of Him and the Kingdom of God. Then, He promises to be with us!

If you are a born-again Believer of Jesus Christ, the Son of the Living God, you are commanded to show others what you already know, which is the way to Jesus and the eternal life that He offers to all. You may ask the question, where do I begin to witness. The answer to that question is found in the word of God which makes it very plain for us, you start where you are or your familiar surroundings. In *Matthew 28,* the nations are people of all races, cultures, rich or poor! Your nation is your household, family members, neighbors, communities, churches, businesses, and jobs! People who you see the most and spend the most time around. *Bloom where you are planted*!

The plans God has for you; your walk with Him; your inner circle, and sharing the gospel, all these include people. People are in the equation of your everyday living on this planet. You cannot get away from them and God does not want you to! God created us to need each other. 'People need people.' We are called to know God, what we have in His Son Jesus Christ and then tell others of the *Good News of the Gospel of Jesus Christ!*

We have heard the phrase, "it is lonely at the top." Used to express someone who is powerful and successful and often have few friends. Like the previous chapter, few friends are good but don't forget to share the love of God with those outside your circle! I've worked on jobs where Christians only witnessed to fellow believer's. Or to those they felt safe to share with. If everyone operated this way, the Kingdom of God would no longer increase! Remember, at the end of the day, it is all Jesus!

When God increases or prospers you, don't forget to reach out to others. Jesus told us that it is hard for those who are rich to enter into the kingdom of heaven. There is no place on earth where people are excluded in the God's kingdom! Do try to avoid the trap of obtaining prosperity and then forgetting others. Don't be high minded. The only top is God, where He reigns, and He looks below and sees people all over the planet whom He loves!

When we work hard, God promises to bless the work of our hands! Work is a major subject of the book of *Deuteronomy*. Work is not limited to a 9-5 job; can be a career, blogger, sports career, nurse, etc. God has promised to bless your work no matter what the plan He has! God wants us to work so that He may bless us and for the benefit of others, the community, and the world.

Deuteronomy 8:18 NKJV, "And you shall remember the LORD your God, for it is He who gives you power to get wealth, that He may establish His covenant which He swore to your fathers, as it is this day."

Do you expect to increase? You should because God is a God of increase. His plans are to prosper you, *Jeremiah 29:11!* As you follow the plan of God, your life will be blessed, it is a certainty! There are so many testimonies of individuals who have become very successful and forgot where they came from. My husband and I often speak on this very topic. We believe in what the Bible says, to not forget God who prospered us nor the people who've helped us along the way. In the book of *Deuteronomy,* Moses is reminding the children of Israel; and good for us too, it is God who has causes you to prosper. That we need to remember our Provider and give thanks!

Deuteronomy 8:12-14 NRSV, "When you have eaten your fill and have built fine houses and live in them, and when your herds and flocks have multiplied, and your silver and gold is multiplied, and all that you have is multiplied, then do not exalt yourself, forgetting the Lord your God, who brought you out of the land of Egypt, out of the house of slavery."

When we possess large estates, beautiful homes, cars, and are engaged in profitable businesses, we are to remember God and be grateful! In this the believing poor have the advantage; they more easily perceive their supplies coming from the Lord, they find less difficulty in simply trusting Him for daily bread. When you are well fed, money in the bank, traveling; it is easier to be prideful and forget all God has done for you! Indeed, God has a plan for your life, but give God all the glory!

The Lord God will never do anything to make Him unnecessary! He is a jealous God and will not share His glory with another! This can easily happen after many years of sweat, a person sees a business, career, research project, child raising, or other work become a success, he or she may have a sense of pride.

As part of His covenant with His people, God gives us the ability to engage in the economy. We need to remember, however, that it *is* a gift of God! When we attribute our success entirely to our abilities and efforts, we forget that God gave us those abilities as well as life itself. We are not self-created. The illusion of self-sufficiency makes us hard-hearted. We can eliminate this by having a proper awareness of our dependency on God and His provision.

God had every intention of leading the children of Israel into prosperity and to enter the Promised Land. The same with us today, God does not change. He has every intention to lead us into prosperity. To increase us and bless our works so that we will give Him the glory and not only have more than enough for ourselves but for those around us. Just like the children of Israel, today, it is up to us whether His plan for our lives is fulfilled! On God's part, He is more than able and capable to do what He promised but it is the error of man to hinder that way!

God also often talks about being a giver! God promises us to bless us as we give and whatever we give, will be given back to us. Not only this, but in abundance.

To bloom where you are planted is a healthy attitude! You start where you are! Look for opportunities to share what God has done for you! Too often, we look for excuses not to share. Such as I'm too shy, I'm not a preacher, I'm not in ministry, and so forth. You see the pattern of self? These are only excuses and you must ask yourself, are you ashamed of God? You do not need a ministry license, or title to bring good news to others! If someone told you a secret of blessings somewhere, most people would tell someone about it. They want to help someone else. This is what God wants us to do, tell the good news of His sending His Son to die for you, to save you and redeem you, so you may have eternal life! If we knew what hell is really like, I do not think we would hesitate to warn, urge, and implore others to come to Jesus!

Luke 2: 13,14 NKJV, "And suddenly there was with the angel a multitude of the heavenly host praising God and saying: Glory to God in the highest, And on earth peace, goodwill toward men!"

Romans 5: 1, 2 NKJV, "Therefore, having been justified by faith, we have peace with God through our Lord Jesus Christ, through whom also we have access by faith into this grace in which we stand, and rejoice in hope of the glory of God."

Having a revelation for ourselves, in order to tell others, that God is at peace with us! He is not mad or angry with us! He has forgiven us through His Son, Jesus Christ! How do you justify this; we look around us and do not see much peace *between* men but the peace the scriptures are referring to are from God *towards* man! God has graciously granted us time (Era of Dispensation) to repent and receive eternal life. The sacrificial offering of Jesus on the Cross for the sin of the whole world was accepted by God the Father! Proof of that acceptance is in the Resurrection of Jesus Christ! When God rose Jesus from the dead, was a symbol of His seal of approval for Jesus being our sacrifice! A person has time before their death on this earth in *this life only* to come to Jesus. After death, comes the judgment! It is too late!

Because we have peace with God, we can witness to others to also be at peace with God and receive Him. Do not harden your hearts but repent and surrender all to Him! Tell of His forgiveness, His kindness, His grace, His mercy, and His love!

Then tell of how we can be at peace with others! We stand equally at the foot of the cross needing a savior. God shows no partially but all have the same opportunity, the same measure of faith to receive, the same covenant promises, and blessings offered! The same forgiveness: it does not depend on race, cultural, status, title, or anything in the earth!

If you are working at a 40-hour job for example, see every job or business as an opportunity to bring the message of hope and love to a person! I know there is a lot of opposition to share but you have a right and you should exercise that right! Be a light and do not be afraid, God is with you wherever you go! Never discount any job as unworthy to share of the goodness of God and all He has done in your life!

By not sharing, we are judging that person and condemning them. Making a choice for them by assuming they will not hear. God only requires we are faithful to share not on the response of the other person. It is up to them, whether they receive or not!

This is your chance! Your job or business could be a dark place spiritually and God not glorified there. It may be a place of oppression and godless people. The company could be full of deceit and lies that you are aware of. Remember, this is your opportunity to shine your light of Jesus in that place! This is why you are there? To be a light! Jesus said the whole do not need a physician but the sick! You are not there to judge nor condemn; this is reserved for the Son of God. But right now, in this era, there is no judgment nor condemnation.

We do not know who will receive if given the chance. They cannot have faith unless they hear! *Romans 10:17 NKJV, "Faith comes by hearing and hearing by the word of God."* Some jobs or assignments will be easier to witness than others. Keep sharing and do not look at their faces or reactions but guard your heart! It is not about you but for the glory of God! Don't get caught up in offence and emotions. Try to stay focus, it is all about what God wills for them to be saved!

Reacting negatively or hurt if person rejects you at first or all together, will only hurt you! They may see unapproachable and rude. You have to remember where you came from and how you also used to believe in error! Extend the grace and give mercy as it has been given to you!

When we think of sharing, we think of being a missionary in a far country and get scared God will send us there. It is a good thing to visit a third world country, or stand on the sidewalk in your city, asking passerby's, do you know Jesus?" Witnessing door to door of people's homes. These are all opportunities, but we miss witnessing to the people we live with and work with every day! People we have the most impact with because we know them; instead, we think we can only be used effectively by going somewhere else.

The important thing to remember is people need God. People need to know that there is a risen Savior who loves, died, and rose again for them! Instead, we want to tell God where we can be used; never realizing we are surrounded by people every day who need to know the message of Christ you now know! This is your field, bloom where you are! It is wrong for us to decide who will receive the message.

God so loved us, He gave and gave all of Himself so we might truly live! God is our #1 supporter! He is cheering us on, believing in us. He will send people, give a word through a song, whatever means necessary to get our attention! Jesus Himself is praying for us all the time! God wants us to mature in the things He has for us and to prosper.

He wants us to rise and soar like an eagle. A wonderful allegory of an eagle, in Christian art, the eagle often represents the resurrection of Christ because the sight of an eagle rising in flight is a powerful one. A baby eagle that learns to soar and glide. When an eagle first leaves the ground, it gains altitude by flapping its wings. The flapping motion causes air to flow faster over the top of the wings, and the bird rises. ... Most eagles have wings that are rather long and wide, to help them soar and glide with less effort. "When it rains, most birds head for shelter; the eagle is the only bird that, in order to avoid the rain, soars above the rain clouds. God wants us to soar like this eagle, above the storms of life with confidence. Unlike the eagle, who usually fly alone, God wants us to affect others around us and fill the Kingdom of God with people!

Isaiah 40:31 NKJV, "But those who wait on the LORD

Shall renew their strength;

They shall mount up with wings like eagles,

They shall run and not be weary,

They shall walk and not faint.

Chapter 13

You Cannot Have a Rainbow Without a Little Rain

Even when you are in the will of God, you can expect some turbulence. Have you ever heard, "God is in control'; "whatever is supposed to happen, will?" Despite popular opinion, according to the word of God, He is not controlling everything nor everyone.

Is God Sovereign? Possessing supreme or ultimate power? A resounding yes, absolutely! God says, "There is no other god, I know not of any!" There is no doubt God stands alone. What needs to be better understood, I believe, is the permissive will of God and what is His sovereign will.

The sovereign (decreed) will of God is God's eternal, foreordained plan, and purpose, which will not change and cannot be thwarted. It includes the salvation plan through Jesus Christ, God's Son; the covenant He made with Jesus for us; His promises; Rapture, Christ's Second Coming and New Earth and New Heaven and much more.

There is what some call God's "permissive will." This is what God allows, even though it is sin. For example, God allowed Adam and Eve to disobey Him. God allows man to reject the gospel, to willfully disobey His laws, to persecute the righteous, and so on. He is not controlling your will. Every person has the freedom to choose, make decisions and to reason. This was given to us by our Creator God. He willingly chose to give us this freedom but even with man's free will, God's purposes will be accomplished!

That being said, God has a plan for your life, is true but His plan for you will not automatically come to pass, not without your cooperation! There have been many who were saved and entered heaven but did not cooperate with God fully in their lives on earth. God was not able to fully implement His plan for them. They lacked faith for God to move in their situations to some degree. For instance, not receiving healing. We can know for a certainty in scripture, this is not God's will for sickness in your life! God promises us a long-satisfied life (*Psalms 91:16*) and Jesus bore all of our sicknesses and diseases, (*Isaiah 53:4, 5*) but the promises are of God are to be received by faith. These promises are all available in Jesus Christ but not all receive. This is man's free will. According to the word of God, it is possible to receive salvation, be born-again but miss the promises of God. Many have entered heaven prematurely. Jesus will receive them, but it is not His perfect will they missed His plan here. He wants to do so much more for us in this life now!

There is a wrong misconception that God needs us to be in heaven. In situations as when a loved one dies; that God is sending them back to watch over their loved ones as angels. God has His angels already to watch over the Believer as messengers. There is no scriptural basis for the thinking some go to heaven to be angels. Nor come back to earth to watch over their loved ones left behind. God created angels and God created man. There is a distinction and He does not switch up once we arrive in heaven. I believe when people think like this, they are wanting to shift the responsibility to God for taking the person prematurely. This may bring some comfort but is not based on truth.

Nevertheless, God wants you to live a long-satisfied life on this earth before entering heaven. It brings God glory to see you receive His promises in this life for which Jesus sacrificed His body and shed His blood for! We don't need the healing, or prosperity or deliverance when were in heaven. We need healing in this fallen world. This is why Jesus came to give us victory in this present world!

God's ultimate goal for every individual is to spend eternity with Him; we could compare to the rainbow. But He knows what we will face before we reach heaven. After Adam sinned and God came looking for Him in the cool of the day to talk with him. Adam was hiding from God because of the sin he had just committed. *God asked him, "What have you done?"* God knew by Adam's reaction of shame, and guilt by hiding, He had sinned. God knew the ramifications of what Adam had done; but clearly Adam had no idea what he had unleased from generation to generation.

From that moment until now, life for every individual is that of struggle and resisting the tricks of the enemy; endeavoring to increase our faith in God and allowing God to walk us through and to the promises! We all love the beauty of the rainbow, but few want to see rainy days that produce that beautiful arch!

We know God made the rainbow and God sends the rain. But man's scientific explanation: the lower the sun in the sky the more of an arc of a rainbow the viewer will see. Rain, fog, or some other source of water droplets must be in front of the viewer. We normally think of rain as a burden or disappointment for our plans. Such as a picnic, field trip, hiking, flying a kite, etc. we can sometimes see rain as an unwelcomed interruption! We rather see the sun shining and the feel the warmth of the sun rays on our faces. We don't want the rain but only days of brightness; puts a smile on our faces and our eyes light up with renewed hope! Foggy days are considered dreary. Few realize that rain is a blessing from God! People in African countries understand this concept very well!

Deuteronomy 28:12 NIV, "The Lord will open the heavens, the storehouse of his bounty, to send rain on your land in season and to bless all the work of your hands. You will lend to many nations but will borrow from none."

There will be rainy days and some fog in your life. Not all days will be bright sunshine. It is how you view the situation and your response. I've known people who confessed they were depressed when the autumn season came, daylight savings time changes or when it has rained for a lengthy period. This is such a waste of your life. You can choose to see the glass half empty or half full! It's all in your perspective.

A healthy outlook I believe is to see every day as beautiful. Even fog can be viewed in the light of beauty and confidence when the fog lifts, how clearer everything will become. This is what I practice. I don't allow a cloudy day to be depressing. It's a day for cooling down the elements, bringing balance to the atmosphere. The rain, to me is God sending refreshing to the land for crops, grass, and shrubbery. Some people like to walk in the rain and feel the rain on their faces as well as the sun! Rain is a sign of refreshing and abundance! Without it, the people, animals, and crops would not survive!

Just like love is not an emotion but a choice! You choose to love or not. How you react to a situation is in your control. God is not making you act a certain way nor can the enemy control you if you will resist him! Your emotions play a very important role in your walking out the plan of God in your life! Does every time it rains, you only see the negativity, or do you seize the day as it is and take advantage of every opportunity. Do you pull the covers over your head and decide to procrastinate, saying tomorrow?

So many people waste time and energy wishing it were Friday or dreading Monday or wanting the sunshine. Time is passing by and this is not a dress rehearsal but the real thing. A believer has life eternal but no other time than this life before death will you have an opportunity to give God glory! We can want to do God's will but don't take steps toward this because of complacency and fear.

There is a difference between desiring and walking out the plan. We endeavor to achieve much but the planning is where you sweat, work hard, sacrifice a lot financially and emotionally! It takes discipline and determination to stick with the plan. Quitting and trying something else will cause confusion and you more than likely will wind up not accomplishing anything. God desires for His people and includes aspects of our salvation such as baptism, service, prayer, wise decisions, and a character that displays the fruit of the Spirit.

Just as the rainbow in Noah's time, after the flood is a sign of a covenant promise of God so is the covenant promise God has with His Son, Jesus Christ for every Believer today! To not destroy life but give life! Everything we need to prosper in this earth is currently available to us! This is good news! Even if you are obeying God as best you can, you can expect problems. There will be growing pains, frustration, and questioning God. It is inevitable! Everyone wants to see the rainbow but complain when there seems to be too much rain. Again, we are creatures of wanting to have quick solutions.

When you're aim is to adhere to the voice and will of God to the best of your ability; you cannot expect life to be smooth sailing. The scriptures say, "All those who live godly shall suffer persecution." This would be a wrong assumption. Especially while obeying God will get the enemies attention and you will have a big old target on your back. It is worth repeating; we live in a fallen world; we do have an enemy and we and others have free wills, who don't always make wise or correct choices. Sometimes, it can seem everything is going wrong. Asking yourself, why so many problems when I'm following where God leads?

The answer to this question is mainly, the enemy will fight the move of God in your life! This is his job, to bring his trickery and deception so you will lose faith in God. The enemy knows faith will open the doors of blessing to flow more easily to you. His main goal, I believe, is to get you to doubt God, as was the case with Eve in the Garden of Eden. If you doubt God too much, you will not have the faith to activate the promises of God already available to you through Jesus!

When you pay for services at the electric company, for your address, a remote-controlled switch connects the power. But if you don't flip the switch inside your home, the lights will remain off. It is available, but you didn't turn it on. Such as the Kingdom of God; Jesus offered His life as payment for our sins. Everything we need is available. God has done His part; the hard part. He gave His life! Ours, is simply to receive (flip the switch). It is as simple as that! The two good to be true news of the gospel! The battle is daily renewing your mind to what you have already received in the spirit!

Someone said it very nicely to me one day this way, "maybe the fact there are problems when following God, means you are moving in the right direction." Instead of thinking we are always, doing something wrong following the path of God, know there are times the struggle is because you are following God as He directed!

You are actually moving in the opposite direction of most people and things are not flowing smoothly. Like rubbing a cat's hair backwards. Most people do not agree with you and in fact, think you are foolish. This can hurt and you can easily become offended but try not to. It is a trick of the enemy to confuse you and cause those spiritual faucets in you to be clogged up and the blessing to be hindered to flow!

I think one of the most captivating pictures to view is the beauty of the rainbow! But do you know what the rainbow symbolizes? It is a sign of hope and promise. When the flood waters receded in Noah's time; God made the rainbow. The promise God will never again cover the earth with waters and destroy every living thing, and the hope of a new beginning! Generally, the rainbow appears after the rain has passed.

Growing up, a frequent prayer request of mine was for God to show me a sign for direction. There was the time, I needed direction trying to decide between three colleges where I had been accepted. I don't remember receiving too many signs as a response to my prayer requests. But what I have received, since then and now is a deep intimate relationship with God and to become acquainted with His presence! God may not give you a sign, but He is leading you in ways you cannot see.

If you are a fairly new believer or a veteran, you may have asked for a sign from God whether you're moving in the right direction. But it seems we are looking for signs too often and not enough trust in the Lord; not enough wanting just His presence! We are prone to frequently be looking for a sign, aren't we? Recently, I was driving down the road, pondering an important decision I needed to make. It's interesting that we as humans don't ask for God's input on every decision, we only seem to want God's handwriting in the sky on certain decisions - the "biggies." Where should I go to school? Whom should I marry? Which job should I take? Or should I change jobs? In each instance, we want God to show us a sign. Any old sign will do. Whether we are reluctant, ambitious, timid, or skeptical, if you are walking with God, you probably want to know how to finish the course! We naturally want God to show us the way! Interestingly, God hardly writes a message in the sky. He never lays a blueprint down. In today's terms, he did not send a fax, an email, or a letter. He does something far better! God promises His presence! Manifested by His Spirit!

Guidance for a Christian comes from our ongoing relationship with God. He wants us to know him. Being guided by Him is a part of that relationship. Signs are temporary; a relationship is permanent. Signs can be misinterpreted, misread, or not seen at all. The devil can send signs and if you don't recognize his strategies, you will be misled. God wants to lead us with every step of our journey, not just in the big important things. And He does that best through relationship. God wants us to know Him and be confident in Him; this is all that matters, isn't it? If we want to know God's will, we must get to know God Himself. Seek Him first and everything else you are concerned about will follow!

> *Matthew 6:33 NKJV, "But seek first the kingdom of God, and His righteousness, and all these things shall be added to you."*

Today, I can see God's hand in my decision regarding which college to attend after graduating high school. I did not see a sign, but the Holy Spirit gently led me in the way I should go. The same city I attended college, is where God had me start ministry for sixteen years. Then after traveling for five years across country and in a foreign country, God brought me and my husband back to that same city! And we're in ministry together! But for me there was no sign. I did not hear the Lord's voice. You just have to follow your heart and know God is with you baby steps! His presence can speak just as loud as a physical human body.

"Corrie ten Boom, the Dutch lady known for her family's hiding of Jews during World War II, in which she was imprisoned, used to say, "Don't wrestle, just nestle." That's what trusting is all about.

A benefit of living in God's presence is that we can snuggle up close to our Heavenly Father, knowing that we can rest confident, secure, and victorious."

When God sends a sign, they are not limited to road signs, directional signs, billboards, or a writing in the sky. But of a still small voice whispering comfortably what to do. Through someone giving you a hug; a song on the radio; a sermon preached; this is *all* God's working! The signs are there, but sometimes we don't pay attention to them. When we are walking with God in the awareness of His presence, His goodness, grace, forgiveness, peace, and joy are signs!

Isaiah 30:21 NKJV, "Your ears shall hear a word behind you, saying, this is the way, walk in it. Whenever you turn to the right hand or whenever you turn to the left."

I know of no one who likes struggles and pain. It does not feel good. But when we go through trials, do not allow bitterness, unforgiveness and resentment to take root. Thank God for His protection and provision through it all! God has warned us many times in the Bible, we would have problems. That He is not taking us out of the problems in this life, but that He will be with us when we go through them! This is one of the most interesting verses in the Bible to me. God says, to *cheer up*! You may be going through some tremendously rough times, but God says, *cheer up*!

John 16:33 NKJV, "These things I have spoken to you, that in Me you may have peace. In the world you will have tribulation; but be of good cheer, I have overcome the world."

Jesus was sitting around talking with His disciples. At one point, He mentions, 'hey guys, I'm leaving you soon.' That He would suffer, and not only that, they too would suffer! Furthermore, Jesus told them that He knew they would all desert Him and run away, leaving Him alone. Jesus reassured the disciples their mourning would turn into rejoicing after a while! Jesus comforted them by telling them and us, in Him we may have peace!

When troubles come, and there is no escaping them, we are to focus on Him. He will keep us in perfect peace! Your focus on Jesus will not necessarily change your circumstances but it will change you and how you handle the challenges! Whether you walk through it with the peace of God or focus on the problem and allow it to stress you! The peace we find in Christ is eternal and will withstand any conditions. In this world you will have trouble. God says, all those who live godly, shall suffer persecution! Rain shall come often but you will not often see the rainbow! Some of the rain will be because the world hates you because it hates God and you do have an enemy! But have courage dear one or be encouraged! Allow the word of God and the comfort of the Holy Spirit to lift you up; to strengthen and establish you! Jesus' words of *cheer up* are meant to embolden us and strengthen our spirit for the fight ahead. *Cheer up* is telling us things will get better! It's not as bad as it seems because this life is temporary. One day when we are with Christ, we won't remember this. Compared to eternity, this is no problem! No worries!

Lastly, Jesus tells us, "I have overcome the world." When Jesus spoke these words, he had not yet faced his trial in the Garden of Gethsemane. He had not yet suffered the mocking, beating, spitting, and torture at the hands of the Jews and the Romans. He had not yet been abandoned by all his followers, betrayed by his Disciples, or denied by one of his closest friends. He had not yet been hung on a cross and forsaken by his Father for the only time in all of eternity. And yet, He replied He had already overcome the world. This was evident in the tense he used (I have, rather than I will). He endured this because He was the Lamb slain since the foundation of the world (Rev 13:8). As his followers, we too can face anything because, in Him, we too have overcome. Take heart and walk out what God has for with joy and for His glory!

Psalms 46:10 AMPC, "Let be and be still and know (recognize and understand) that I am God, I will be exalted among the nations! I will be exalted in the earth."

"Let be," and "be still," two phrases that are for almost everyone, quite difficult to do! When you are in fear and frantic, you cannot sense the peace of God nor hear His voice. When your emotions are calm, you are more able to hear God speaking! One evening while driving, I missed my turn and for some reason, I became very afraid. I usually don't react like I did that night due to missing a turn in traffic! Crying out to God for help, I was so frustrated trying to find the signs to get back on track. I could not hear God or feel His leading in anyway. Finally, I found the road, I needed, and it was pitch dark now. When I returned home, I did not understand, why I was so afraid. God had me understand eventually through prayer, I could not hear His voice because of the fear. If I had of quieted down, relaxed and prayed with a discerning ear, I would have heard Him better! I would have heard Him tell me, I'm sure, don't worry, it's not a problem or this is the way to go! At the time, I began to meditate on what happened so I would not react that way again. Realizing now the root of my problem was not trusting God. I needed to be still and recognize who God was in this situation and what happened that caused my fear to escalate from a simple problem.

A few years later, I would make my first trip across country alone. It proved beneficial for that successful journey to see my situation as small and God as BIG! If I could not see God's leading in a small miss turn in traffic, how could I make a trip across country by myself?

God is talking, but your fear is talking much louder. God is not trying to talk over your fear, He waits until you are calmer. Have you seen a person who is hysterical, let's say waking up from a bad dream? You're trying to wake them up and let them know it is okay now! But they are still half asleep. At one point, after you keep shaking them, they hear you and wake up! Suddenly, everything is put into right perspective for them! Now that person dreaming is more alert and can hear you!

It may be raining and maybe a little foggy, but put into the proper perspective, it is just rain and depending on how you view that rainy day is your victory or defeat! The fog will disappear, and everything will be clear and beautiful again! It is not a real problem. Rain is a blessing for replenishing! Your problems do not determine your outcome with God!

Psalms 126:5 NKJV, "Those who sow in tears, shall reap in joy."

They that sow in tears shall reap in joy. Hence, present distress must *not* be viewed as if it would last forever; it is not the end, by any means, but only a means to the end. Sorrow is our sowing; rejoicing shall be our reaping!

See the beauty in the rain. See beauty in the struggle. The rainbow when it appears will be that much more beautiful! Live each day with appreciation. Don't wait until the finished project, the rainbow. See God in the little things. In the problems, see God working it out for your good and His glory!

Chapter 14

Everyday Miracles

Romans 12:2 NKJV, "And do not be conformed to this world, but be transformed by the renewing of your mind, that you may prove what is that good and acceptable and perfect will of God."

How do you get to the place where you can see the miraculous happen in and through you? It starts with the renewing of your mind. It is not just knowing additional information or positive thinking. It doesn't matter if you 'know more' and therefore you will become a better person. It is not dwelling too much on negative thoughts instead of positive. To renew your mind is to test what is truth and what isn't. The process of exchanging the lies for the truth. Exchanging your natural way of thinking for God's way of thinking.

The Bible tells us the ***lies*** are, "I can't change"; "I have to earn God's grace"; "God has given up on me"; "Today is going to be horrible day"; "More money is going to make me happy, etc." The ***truths*** according the God's word is, "I am the righteousness of God in Christ Jesus," "I can do all things through Christ which strengthens me," or "Thanks be to God who always cause me to triumph in Christ Jesus."

God's word is the instrument; your mind is the field and

the Spirit of God is the power to help you change your thinking and distinguish what is truth or lie to you. So, if you desire to be transformed and live like Christ, then you must give yourself to the pursuit of renewing your mind. What images or thoughts are running in your mind that is causing you to act in a certain way? What are you allowing to be projected?

This will help you understand what you've already received through the *Finished Work of the Cross of Jesus!* Everything we need to live victoriously in this life has been given to us and they are in Christ Jesus!

> 2 Peter 1:3-4 KJV, *"According as his divine power hath given unto us all things that pertain unto life and godliness, through the knowledge of him that hath called us to glory and virtue: Whereby are given unto us exceeding great and precious promises: that by these ye might be partakers of the divine nature, having escaped the corruption that is in the world through lust."*

To know this truth is to have knowledge in God's word and believing what God says in His word. A miracle is a surprising and welcome event that is not explicable by natural or scientific laws and is therefore considered to be the work of a divine agency. Miracles generally happen in the time of crisis! Healing, divine intervention of dangers seen and unseen, or financial needs to name a few. God intervenes to bless you with supernatural abundance or deliverance from a harmful situation at the time you need it!

But God doesn't want you to live from crisis to crisis. He wants you to walk in the *everyday blessings* He has provided through His Son! From *glory to glory*! Live your life expecting miracles to happen all the time! But walk in the blessings of God continually! Miracles are temporary but blessings are permanent. Live your life expecting good changes to occur as you follow God! This is faith! I have seen so many miracles in my life; now I look for them! At the same time, I am walking in the blessing He has provided! God wants to bless us so much! I believe He is looking for opportunities to draw you closer to Him!

In following the plan of God for your life, stop and smell the roses! It is an easy trap, trying to get to the next place in our lives, next job, new career move, we miss what is happening every day in plain view! All too often, we are not discerning and recognize after the fact. God wants you to ask and believe Him for the answer. He is able to do far more than you can imagine.

Jeremiah 33:3 NKJV, "Call to Me, and I will answer you, and show you great and mighty things, which you do not know."

A miracle that prevented me from a bad accident happened as I exited an interstate highway. A driver speeding too fast to stop behind me, looked as if they were going to rear end my car.

Suddenly, the car stopped and smoothly veered to the side of the entrance ramp. It looked as if, and I believe so, someone took hold of the car (angel) and gently moved it to the side. I witnessed the whole thing in my rear-view mirror. The other driver was obviously fine. I began to praise the Lord and continued to as I entered the store of my destination. When I drove back on the highway within the hour, on the back of a tractor trailer in front of me, were the words, 'God Loves You.' God prevented a bad accident for me. Thank you, Jesus!

Another miracle where God prevented me from an accident were with deer. While driving, I saw deer leaping in the path of my car. This startled me of course and caused me to tap the brakes. As soon as I did, three deer leaped in front of my vehicle, barely missing me! God alerted me to the deer jumping before it actually happened. They would have hit my car, had I not stopped!

I've laid hands on the sick and they did recover! I've been in a jeep on a Safari, where there was no fence and suddenly an elephant appears! Praying in the spirit, the elephant looked as if it was pondering whether to charge at us. Then after a short time, it moved backwards and walked away! I've seen what the power of fervent prayer will do for others and when I pray as I pray with expectation! Expecting miracles!

Sometimes we are so involved in ourselves and our needs that we fail to recognize the everyday miracles and blessing happening all around us. If you as a parent, were only looking forward to your child's first day at school, first date, first car or first anything; we would miss the first little things, roll over, stand up, walk, or talk. There are significant more little things than events that happen in our lives. If we only were happy during the events, our lives in between those times, would be miserable and not fulfilling! I have been too am guilty of this; waiting for what lies ahead. It is especially difficult after God has given you a revelation of something in your life, whether a ministry, a book, a wedding and so forth. You can become too anxious! In preparing for your wedding, if you only are happy when the officiant announces you are now married, what about the courting, dating, announcement of marriage, engagement period and wedding planning! What about the marriage itself! You can only be joyful when an event is taking place?

Philippians 4:6, 7 NKJV, "Be anxious for nothing but in everything by prayer and supplication with Thanksgiving let your request be made known to God and the peace of God which surpasses all understanding will guard your hearts and minds through Christ Jesus."

This is a scripture I meditate on frequently! This verse teaches us to not allow worry or stress to take away our peace of mind while waiting on something. To cast all our cares on Jesus for He cares for us. But that no matter the situation, talk to God about whatever! The peace will come when you pray. Then leave it with God but safeguard your heart and mind purposing to trust Him. Lastly, expect God to answer clearly for you! If you need a miracle, don't be afraid to ask for it and believe!

We have to learn to be content and thankful every day throughout the day! See the wonders of the Lord, in His creation. Take a drive and see the beauty of God's nature! The landscape of flowers, greenery of the trees or autumn color. Enjoy the sunrise or sunset; the colors lighting up the sky as a new day dawn! Take a drive to the beach and hear the roaring of the waves yet the gentleness and quietness of its sound. The walks where the sand digs in between your toes and cools them from the burning sun rays! What about the wind, a warm not too brisk day where the wind is blowing your hair around into your face blocking your view.

The Bible tells us to think more positive thoughts but to also change your thinking. It can be a beautiful day even while it is raining outside. Rain does not obscure the beauty of a day.

If I, by writing this book, where only excited with the beginning and consumed with just finishing it, I would miss the enjoyment of every chapter, of the research and revisiting the events of my testimony. How the Lord ministered to me in writing this book, with each paragraph! We miss so much, not stopping to consider, think or ponder. To take a deep breath! This can lead to a life of regrets and where has time gone? When we die, we want to leave memories not unfulfilled dreams!

Stop, take inventory, and count your many blessings! Be grateful and appreciative of the blessing we take for granted! As I write this, the world is at a place of having to stop and consider many things! Some have not spent time together in years that we are forced to having to do now! It is challenging for some, but others are rediscovering, I hope, their roots! Our lives are not to be self-centered, where we don't care for other's.

Focusing only on ourselves will lead to a victim mentality and you will murmur and complain. This will also give you a bad attitude towards others and God! Nothing will be good enough for you until you get what you think you want. Until you have the money you are looking to achieve, the job or status. Never satisfied even after your accomplishments. Always wanting more! Saying, I will not be complete or happy until I have a baby, a husband. If you are not careful, even those things will only be a temporary joy for you.

God delights when we are receiving His blessings, as a good Father would! These blessings are here for us to enjoy! A good parent wants to see his children blessed and happy! That same parent will not be happy if the child is ungrateful and unthankful! No matter where I am in my walk with God, I try to live each day being thankful and telling God thank you in so many ways. To recognize what He has done for me and those I love! In fact, I wake up giving thanks! One day, these material possessions will be gone but God is eternal and our life with Him if we receive.

As we pray, God will connect us with individuals we don't know. Sometimes, a miracle will take place. Remember, we rise by lifting others! A smile can make a person's day, whether they tell you or not. You don't know what they are going through! I was once on a job where God gave me the opportunity with a group of wonderful ladies to have a Bible study. We saw awesome miracles happen many times throughout the years! We all had families outside of the job but took advantage of the opportunity to help someone else receive their miracles through prayers offered on the job!

For example, man who after years of running from God, surrendered his life to Jesus! Turns out many of his relatives had been praying for him for quite some time. He shared he comes from a family background of Christians and how he knows the scriptures very well. He said He had been running from the Lord and was not ready to receive the word. But, had gotten to a place in his life where he was broken and ready to surrender to the Lord Jesus Christ! He had finally come to the end of himself, had stopped running and knelt down and prayed for the Lord Jesus to come into his heart and be his Lord and Savior! I later told him it was all those prayers that were over his head! He was a different man, more peaceful, joyful, and full of gratitude unto the Lord for His forgiveness. His heart was no longer hardened but humbled!

Another testimony was when an employee's son of the company, was involved in a horrible head-on-collision close to his high school graduation, that nearly ended his life! Our prayer group pressed in and asked others to do the same. Doctors were not giving this young man much hope and if he did come out of the coma, they were concerned about brain damage. He endured multiple surgeries in addition to physical therapy.

God had a miracle with his name on it. One day, I ran into the father and this young man, who was in a wheelchair. After talking with him a little bit, he quickly agreed for me to lay hands on him in the store for healing. The young man was totally receiving and shared he was believing for a miracle and praying hard for it! Also, he is a Believer in Jesus Christ! At this moment, God led me to tell this young man He would indeed heal him, (*because of his faith*) and that he would walk normally again without the wheelchair. This young man confidently and assuredly responded he received that and believed Jesus would heal him completely!

Within two weeks after this meeting, it was my delight to see this young man come to our job with his dad walking (no wheelchair, crutches nor cane) into the building with a slight limp! Shortly after this, we heard the man's son was graduating from high school on time with his classmates and planning on going to college. A true miracle!! Praise the Lord!

Some say miracles do not happen today. If that were true, how did you get saved? Salvation is a miracle. It is the supernatural work of God! This explains why a pregnancy is defined as a *"miracle "*. It encompasses not only those changes that are visible, on a physical level; but also, and above all, more hidden changes, on an emotional and psychological level and of course concerning the growth of the fetus in the womb. Look up, see clearly what the Lord is doing today!

Miracles glorify God! God not only expects us to use our supernatural abilities He has given us, but miracles give God the glory!

Mark 16: 17,18 NKJV, "And these signs will follow those who believe: In My name they will cast out demons; they will speak with new tongues; they will take up serpents; and if they drink anything deadly, it will by no means hurt them; they will lay hands on the sick, and they will recover."

Signs and wonders are for the purpose of validating the Word of God, which is what will change people's lives. God's Word is what changes people's lives, but how do you get them to believe that it really is God speaking? Well, this is the purpose of miracles.

When you minister to someone about them receiving healing, we demonstrate it by speaking over them in the name of Jesus. When they receive their healing, it validates that it is God. Miracles aren't going to change people, but they will cause them to believe the word you've spoken is the Word of God. Including casting out demons or taking up anything deadly and not being hurt. Jesus preached and taught the word of God and then demonstrated in power what He said! The Bible says, "the Lord working with them and confirming the word through the accompanying signs." There are so many other examples in the Bible!

1 Corinthians 2:1 NIV, "When I came to you, I did not come with eloquence or human wisdom as I proclaimed to you the testimony about God. For I resolved to know nothing while I was with you except Jesus

Christ and him crucified. [3] I came to you in weakness with great fear and trembling. [4] My message and my preaching were not with wise and persuasive words, but with a demonstration of the Spirit's power, [5] so that your faith might not rest on human wisdom, but on God's power."

Jesus did not come emphasizing and using words only but in demonstration of the Spirit and power, so their faith would stand in the power of God not in the wisdom of man.

John 11:43 NIV, "When he said this, he then called in a loud voice, "Lazarus, come forth!" Lazarus comes out of the tomb alive, his hands and feet wrapped with strips of linen, and a cloth around his face. ***Jesus*** *says to the bystanders, "Take off the grave clothes and let him go."*

Jesus had emphasized prior to raising Lazarus from the dead, that He is the Resurrection and the Life. Anyone believing in Him, though he may die, he shall live! Jesus also delayed going to Lazarus to heal him two more days, for He had heard Lazarus was only sick at this time. Jesus said, *"And I am glad for your sakes that I was not there, that you may believe. Nevertheless, let us go to him."* Jesus had told them, this sickness was not unto death, but for the glory of God, that the Son of God may be glorified through it. Jesus was making it clear; He had the power to raise you from the dead and if you believe in Him, the power to give you eternal life with Him!

Mark 2: 5-10 NKJV, "When Jesus saw their faith, He said to the paralytic, Son, your sins are forgiven you. And some of the scribes were sitting there and reasoning in their hearts, why does this Man speak blasphemies like this? Who can forgive sins but God alone? But immediately, when Jesus perceived in His spirit that they reasoned thus within themselves, He said to them, why do you reason about these things in your hearts? Which is easier, to say to the paralytic, 'Your sins are forgiven you,' or to say, 'Arise, take up your bed and walk'? But that you may know that the Son of Man has power on earth to forgive sins"—He said to the paralytic,

In the example of this scripture, Jesus heals a paralytic man.

Here, Jesus is demonstrating His ability and authority to not only heal but forgive sins! God is a God of miracles! These same miracles are available today. Jesus went back to heaven, but He lives in every Believer and the Holy Spirit dwells in every Believer working through us signs and wonders! *Hebrews 13:8 NKJV, "Jesus Christ the same yesterday, and today, and forever."* If you need a miracle, it is available today! Get into God's word and see how it worked for other people and apply those things in your life.

Chapter 15

Fulfilling God's Will, Get Off the Couch!

Habakkuk 2:3 AMPC, "For the vision is yet for an appointed time and hastens to the end [fulfillment]; it will not deceive or disappoint. Though it tarry, wait [earnestly] for it, because it will surely come; it will not be behind schedule on its appointed day."

What God has spoken in your heart, will one day happen, if you do not lose heart. If you persevere and follow where He leads; not always perfectly, but to the best of your ability! God is able to get you where you need to be in order for His word to come to pass in your life! In the process of the fulfilled will of God, He will speak various matters to you. **Projects** He wants you to partake of. **Partnerships** He wants you to form. **Places** He wants you to go. **People** He wants you to connect with! With each act of obedience or step of faith, hearing His voice will be clearer and bring you closer to your destiny. Knowing His ways will be not be a mystery. Trusting Him will be not hard at all.

God called me to be a preacher and Bible teacher. After the calling, there was a period before my trial sermon date was scheduled; a ceremony to publicly announce my calling! When that day was revealed to me by my pastor, I was very excited, and at the same time, peaceful! God had done a work in me until that point. When God gives you His plan, He is telling you the end result. There is a good chance, He will not go into depth of what the process will look like before the vision comes to pass. He knows it will be overwhelming for you or cause unnecessary fear. He is still preparing you to fit the vision. He sees you will be successful but in the natural, your character needs adjustment. Your attitude needs fine tuning.

God doesn't call the qualified. He qualifies the called! Someone who is qualified is officially recognized as being trained to perform a particular job; certified. For example, a "newly qualified nurse." But in the Kingdom of God, He sees your end from the beginning. He sees what you will be and then calls you. Then He trains you in that calling. Every area of your life encompasses that calling. He connects you to divine opportunities. He opens doors that no mere man can shut. God sets you on a path where the calling itself will lead you closer to the end result. You will have to walk by faith! Inevitably, there will be road blocks by the enemy and sometimes intentional detours to throw you off track. But God is aware beforehand of all these and knows how to connect you back on the right roads.

Similar to a GPS, but spiritually, it is God's Positioning System. Your GPS has to be connected with the power on. It is powerless without the connection to the satellite and battery charged. With

God, it does no good, if you are not connected to the Vine (John 15:5). Jesus is the Vine and we are the branches. There will be no power!

2 Timothy 1:14 NKJV, "That good thing, which was committed to you, keep by the Holy Spirit who dwells in us."

"God gives us the deposit of the Holy Spirit, and once you have the Holy Spirit within you, you're connected to God, and your God Positioning System is ready to guide you".

You have to want to move forward!

Isaiah 45:2 NKJV, "I will go before you and make the crooked places straight."

Even without the GPS, if you're driving a car and want to get to a destination, you have to start the car and move forward to that destination. As you go, God will direct you. He is much better than the GPS! God existed before the GPS and before maps. He guided the wise men by His created star to where the baby Jesus was with His parents. God can direct you because He sees all and watches over you! The vision starts after God speaks. Once the will of God is known, He requires a response from you! I've heard people say they will not move until God tells them where to go. This is not faith. Faith requires action and as you go forward, God will make those crooked places straight.

You may be one who resists change. It is unnerving and

frightening for you. *God is a God of change and the Holy Spirit has come to bring change.* This is what renewing you mind is all about. Changing your mind, your old way of thinking. Repentance is about changing your ways to what God is telling you. We have to resist the fear of change! In order to embrace all God has for us, we cannot stay the same. *God will take you just like you are, broken and destitute but He loves you too much to leave you that way!*

Proverbs 19:21 ESV, "Many are the plans in the mind of a man, but it is the purpose of the Lord that will stand."

It is good to make your own plans the best you can, but we must be open to the leading of the Holy Spirit. And open to the Holy Spirit erasing our plans in some ways to fit the will of God for your life!

To say I was not qualified to preach or teach when God called me, is an understatement. It was five years after God placed me in various ministries to work from the day, He called me to preach. It was two years from the calling, I shared with my pastor of my calling to the scheduled sermon. A total of five years from the time I began working in ministry to that day. Even now after twenty-six years of ministry, I haven't arrived, but I've left. I won't arrive until I reach heaven with Jesus!

We can get so excited when God reveals anything to us, we forget about the process and timing! We fail to recognize the rest of the scripture, says the vision will happen at an appointed time. The scripture verse in Habakkuk drawn is a beautiful illustration of the vision. What it will look like when it is finished or completed. What God does not tell us, is what takes place after the vision is spoken and when it is fulfilled. He just tells us the end and walks us through the process. For if we knew the trials, persecutions and challenges that awaited because of the vision, it would overwhelm us! We may fight God on every hand because of fear. We are human and we want the mountaintop experiences, but we want them without the valleys. God is teaching us Christlike character while we wait.

Psalms 32:8 NKJV, "I will instruct you and teach you in the way you should go; I will guide you with My eye."

Again, every spoken word requires an act of obedience. If you love God, obey Him. Don't constantly disobey God's will for your life and say that you love Him! Love is not a feeling, it's an act of the will, and obedience to what is right. And the good news is, if you obey Him, He works on your behalf to lead you into the greatest life possible! If you could only see things from God's perspective, you would not have any trouble being obedient and trusting Him.

God, for example, may tell you one day you will travel to Spain for a missionary journey. He leaves out: the exact date (could take years from when He said it); all the people involved to get you to that point; how you will get the provision; or what you are to do when you arrive, and so on and so on. What will be your answer to

God? What will you say? How will you begin to prepare for going to Spain?

James 2:17 NKJV, "Faith by itself, if it does not have works, is dead."

Simple mental agreement is not enough. "Knowledge" is not "trust." Salvation does not come when a person agrees to the *facts* of Christ's life, death, and resurrection. Such a "belief" requires no response, no action. In the book of James, he points out that merely claiming something does not make the claim true. A person who says, "I believe," but does nothing to support such a belief, *does not actually believe* what they have claimed.

Therefore, what steps would you now take to prepare for your missionary journey to Spain? May I suggest, reading books on the country; taking Spanish lessons if you don't already speak the language; fundraisers; researching climate; culture in general; estimating the cost of ticket; looking for hosts for living quarters to connect with and so much more. Keep in mind, you still do not know when yet, but you heard God and now your faith makes you take steps toward when the time comes! As you take these necessary steps, your mind will be acclimatized to where you are going. God will place you connection with people who have already been where you are believing to go. These people will be sounding boards for you in encouragement, recommendations, other contacts, suggestions, or wise counselling! Your everyday choices will be geared to that very plan.

There was a man in the Bible, who had an infirmity for 38 years. He laid at a pool named Bethesda. Waiting for someone to throw him in for healing. Scripture tells us an angel went down a certain time and would stir the water and whoever stepped in first would be healed. The man with the infirmity told how no one would put him in the pool and how others would get in front of him, *John 5:1-16.* But at last, his time had come and this man with the infirmity for 38 years was healed by the Lord Christ Jesus himself! Notice how the man never got in the pool for his healing, (he wasn't able), but Jesus stopped by to see him one day and spoke to his affliction and said be healed, rise, take up your bed and walk!

This tells us that the man had an infirmity for 38 years but does not tell us how long he waited by the pool of Bethesda. We just know that he waited for a long time. The Lord drew my attention to this man 's story. You can be waiting for a long time and others are seemingly getting blessed before you. God is teaching you how to wait. To be still and know that He is God. Also notice that God used this man's waiting for His glory and this man's testimony was written in the Holy Scriptures! Not that He caused this affliction; for sickness does not come from God but from satan. But He showed up when this man needed Him! His waiting was not in vain, even though it probably seemed like it for a long time. Because when God shows up, no matter how long the wait, you will not be ashamed for waiting on Him, *Isaiah 49:23.*

I am sure this afflicted man in *John 5* after receiving the great blessing of total healing no longer cared how long he waited to achieve it. This makes the blessing that much sweeter when it comes! And you appreciate the blessing more because you are more grateful! Much like, I have heard, having a baby. You forget the labor pains after the child is born and rejoice in the blessing of the newborn life in your arms. This is just like the promises of God. You will not regret when the blessing come! You will forget the pain and what you went through! The Bible tells us:

Romans 8:18 NKJV, "The sufferings of this present time shall not be compared to the glory that shall be revealed in us."

Waiting on God is not just something we should do, but God wants us to wait on Him with a good attitude. An attitude of gratitude and cheerfulness. God often speaks of having a cheerful heart when giving and when waiting. While we wait on God, He wants us to have a servant attitude of trust and faith. He wants us to serve while we wait (trust) in Him.

Mark 9:33-35 NKJV, "if anyone desires to be first, he shall be last of all and servant of all."

In your calling from God, He may give you a leadership position or title. It is okay, as long as you understand, it is not just about titles in the Kingdom of God, but it is about serving. Nothing wrong with titles, I have them and they are gifts administered in the church. If God gives you one, wear it honorably but humbly!

Do not be afraid to get out of the boat. Be a water walker! The disciple, Apostle Peter, actually walked on the water going to Jesus! He took his eyes off Jesus and began to sink. Peter is criticized for this, but my point of view is, how many people have we heard who actually walked on water except Jesus Himself? To me, Peter had tremendous faith! Faith to get out of the boat. Most of us would hesitate, in the middle of the ocean and get out of our comfort zone and believe to not swim but walk on the water! There were countless times, I know if I had not obeyed God, I would not have the blessing and miracles in my life now. You cannot know what is on the other side of your obedience.

My second overseas trip for missions was by myself; me and God! I was a little scared but mostly peaceful. It is not that fear is not present sometimes when obeying God; but there is more faith that counteracts the fear and you move forward! I am learning God is greater than my fear. Fear is an enemy! You can be afraid and have faith at the same time. Try not to allow your fears to hinder you from living an adventuresome life with God! When I look back, I see how fear is 'false evidence appearing real.'

Before my marriage, as a single, I acted alone. I greatly desired and endeavored to have support but was not overly successful there.

You cannot wait for people! It is always great to have a support base, people or someone who believes in you. But at the time there is no one present, decide to go forward with God! Personally, this is my lifestyle and I have never regretted it! In fact, my life was enriched abundantly, when I obeyed God!

At the time when Jesus needed His disciples the most, they left Him alone. They abandoned Him but Jesus said, He was not alone, for the Father was with Him! In your greatest test or getting out of the boat, know that God is with you. He is more real to you than a person who is capable of letting you down! He lives in every Believer and you are in His presence at all times. He is very much mindful of you and will not abandon you!

Ephesians 3:20, 21 NKJV, "Now to Him who is able to do exceedingly abundantly above all that we ask or think, according to the power that works in us.

Now, God is not able to bring abundantly more good things in your life, if you will not cooperate with Him! Everything is not automatic! God is only able to do exceedingly abundantly above all according to your cooperation. He will not force it. Surrendering your plan to Him and allowing Him to give you His plan! Cannot have two visions. Two visions are division!

Hebrews 11:7 NIV, "By faith Noah, when warned about things not yet seen, in holy fear built an ark to save his family. By his faith he condemned the world and became heir of the righteousness that is in keeping with faith."

And speaking of boats, what about an ark? Noah moved with fear, and it had never rained, nor did he know what rain looked like, but He believed God! Noah was a man of faith called by God to preach! God saw his faith and told him the plan. That men were continually evil in their hearts and He would end all life. Because of Noah's faith, He would spare his life and that of his families. Along with every kind of species (male and female) to start again with replenishing the earth of the same kind. God's plan was to cause waters (rain) over the entire earth to flood everything. Even the top of the mountains would be covered. No one could hide there! God told Noah to build an Ark and He told Noah how to build the Ark with the exact measurements and equipment needed! God supplied everything but Noah had to build. Let's visualize how long this actually is by comparing it to items we are familiar seeing.

- The Ark was twice as long as an early Boeing 747-100B airliner.
- It would take nearly one and a half football fields to equal the Ark's length.

Noah had to cooperate, or he would have died with everyone else. Because of God's mercy and grace, God gave Noah time to build the Ark. The floods did not come until Noah had finished.

God waited patiently until Noah finished and then judgment came. God is longsuffering with us and not willing anyone should perish. Today, people take His silence to mean; He is dead, not real or will not do anything. His silence is love and longsuffering and kindness for us to give us time to repent.

It took Noah at least one hundred years to complete the building of the Ark! It was a big boat that needed to house a lot of animals! During this time, Noah preached, it was going to rain! To repent! God would have accepted anyone who repented and come into the Ark with Noah and his family, but none did! The people had never seen rain (including Noah) and did not believe him. They must have thought Noah was crazy! No one aided him in the building of the Ark (*except maybe his family*), but all just ignored him. Because if they had believed, they would put action with their faith and help Noah build the Ark.

Noah believed the plan of God and trusted God! He took acts of faith with godly fear and reverence to God to proceed as quickly as possible! He worked and he preached to let everyone know what God was going to do. If Noah had not moved in the direction of what God told him; picking up the materials provided to start working, he and his family would have perished. His faith required action. God equips us with the necessary tools to get started. We have all the provision needed for the journey. God is not holding you accountable for what you don't know. God is a good God and just! In His mercy, He first warns us before judgment.

While the people in Noah's time did not hear God speak, they heard Noah preach to them from God! Try not to get caught up in others unbelief. Each of us have to give an account of what we did in our bodies in this earth one day standing before God! If you hear Him, it is enough for your walk with God. You are only responsible for yourself, not someone else.

Adam and Eve

He first warned Adam not to eat of the tree of knowledge of good and evil. Adam then informed his wife, Eve. God warned them and they disobeyed. They died spiritually with fallen natures and bodies. Physically, they died; not immediately but aged from that moment. Eventually dying and as we do today.

Genesis 2:15-17, "The Lord God took the man and put him in the Garden of Eden to work it and take care of it. And the Lord God commanded the man, "You are free to eat from any tree in the garden; but you must not eat from the tree of the knowledge of good and evil, for when you eat from it you will certainly die."

The Ten Commandments

Exodus 20 God warned children of Israel before reprimanding them.

Prophets and Priests

God warned in the Old Testament through His chosen men and women before judgment.

Jesus Christ, the Son of God

God warn us today through His ministers by witnessing for a space of time (Era if Dispensation) before Judgment Day! If you are born again, God warns you by the leading of the Holy Spirit who lives in every Believer.

Your faith requires taking steps toward what you believed you heard! It indicates a willingness to go and an expectation that you will receive what you were told!

If someone told you that if you drive to XYZ and there would be one million dollars waiting for you. They just required you to come and pick up. Let's say it is a legitimate offer. How many would be willing to go and take steps toward achieving that end goal. It doesn't matter what obstacles arose; car stalling; can't take off from work; do not have a car. How many would do whatever is possible to receive this natural gift! How much more should we be excited and anticipating spiritual gifts that are eternal from our Heavenly Father who Created all things!

Your reality should be more real to you spiritually than in natural things of the world! It is due to the fact we are carnal. We only see with our natural eyes. This world will perish and the things in it, but God is eternal and only what He gives us will last!

Deuteronomy 28:12 NKJV, "to bless all the work of your hand."

It is time to get off the couch! God promises to bless the works of our hands! Adam had to tend and keep the Garden—to work it and take care of it. In the Garden, his work was fruitful and productive. From the beginning, God told us to work and He would bless. A child when they learn to walk take baby steps and the parent is with them taking care until they walk by themselves. How much more, God, as you take baby steps of faith, God is with you and taking care of you! He cannot fail you!

Chapter 16

Discipleship

Discipleship in the Christian sense is the process of making someone become like Christ. The disciple of Christ is to become like Christ in everything. The primary purpose of Jesus coming to the world was to establish the Kingdom of God through his death. **Discipleship in Relationship**…Just as their relationships with Christ and each other played a key factor in the spiritual maturity of Peter, James, John, and the other Disciples, it is also important for us to keep in mind the role that our relationships play in our discipleship journey. The term "disciple" which generally means "one who engages in learning through instruction from another, pupil, apprentice" or in religious contexts such as the Bible, "one who is rather constantly associated with someone. God calls us to first win the lost to Him and then to disciple.

Mark 8:34-38 NKJV, "Whoever desires to come after Me, let him deny himself, and take up his cross, and follow Me."

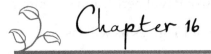

Our lives are to become a Disciple of Jesus Christ and then disciple others to become one. This scripture verse in Mark is saying to deny yourself is not hating yourself but to give full control of your life to Christ. Dead to your own will and ready to accept whatever costs are involved in a life of complete Christian commitment. Jesus teaches us in the word of God how to win the lost and then teach them. In *(Matthew 4:18-22),* Jesus called His first disciples, *"Follow Me, and I will make you fishers of men."NKJV* He called them and then they became converted.

He prayed and was in close communion with God the Father. Jesus led a lifestyle of prayer and dependence on God. Choosing His disciples from that prayer. When God told Him whom to choose, Jesus went looking for them. Those He called, they accepted and followed Him! Then Jesus invested in them; time, prayers, advice, counsel, love, teaching and training them about the Kingdom of God. About whom God is and what He had provided for them! Jesus taught them how to renew their minds to God's word!

A person who has been incarcerated (criminal or enslaved for whatever reason) for a long period of time, may need to be rehabilitated. It can be difficult for an offender or person imprisoned to be reintegrated back into the community. They may need training and time. A delivered person from an addiction needs therapy, a person with an illness may need to be trained on mobility skills. They are being taught how to be restored to what is considered normal in society.

God sent Jesus to restore mankind back to His original intent from the beginning. To get back what the enemy had deceived us out of; our rights, promises, blessings, and inheritance! We were lost and without hope in this world! God sent Jesus to save man from eternal damnation! We were held captive by sin and separated from God! We owe Jesus everything! He came to reconcile us back to God!

Luke 4:18 NKJV, "The Spirit of the L*ORD is upon Me, because He has anointed MeTo preach the gospel to the poor; He has sent Me to heal the brokenhearted, To proclaim liberty to the captives And recovery of sight to the blind, To set at liberty those who are oppressed"*

When you become a Believer, we are to invest ourselves in helping others to know the good news we know. A Disciple is an obedient follower of Jesus Christ who is actively engaged in making disciples by teaching obedience to everything Jesus commanded in His word. Discipleship is what every Believer should have a heart and compassion for.

Whatever your area of gifting, showing a spark of hope to somebody else can be extremely rewarding for any individual. We cannot rule certain people out by picking and choosing who will be saved based on how we like that person. God alone knows who will be saved and who will not receive Him. That is not for us to try and figure out. Even those difficult people." You know those unlovable people whom God loves too. Jesus is the Savior of the world and anyone can come to Him not just the people we select. He loves us all the same, Believer or non-Believer. Having the desire to disciple, you first must have compassion. If we would open our hearts to all different people, we will find that God is able and will use us to lead that person to Him and change their lives around. Jesus says if we will be available and willing and lift Him up, He will draw them unto Himself.

John 12:32 NKJV, "If I am lifted up from the earth, will draw all peoples to Myself."

1 John 4:7,8 NKJV, "Beloved let us love one another: for love is of God and everyone that loves is born of God and knows God...for God is love."

You can begin to start letting God's love flow through you to minister to other people. You have the power and the anointing of God in you and God can flow through you to someone else. Having an awareness of what is already on the inside of you is important. You will begin to share with others your excitement, give testimonies of what God has done in your life, and as a result some people will receive help. For example, you can allow the love of God to flow through you to another person. It is not the same as an attraction or fleshly desire, but supernatural from the very heart of God!

Love is a necessity in discipleship. Love is a choice, not an emotion. *1 Corinthians 13:4-8,* love is not envious, love is long suffering, kind, selfless, bears all things; love endures. You are not loving a person based off what they can do for you but unconditional love that

Jesus gives! When Jesus was hanging on the cross, He saw some of His torturers and accusers. He loved them anyway. People He had healed and helped. People He had fed when they were hungry. But He did not enjoy the agonizing whip lashes across His back (*forty stripes*). He didn't embrace becoming sin for mankind as pleasurable. Jesus endured the cross because He saw the pleasure of us receiving eternal life! He willing chose to do it for each person! He saw past the suffering and willingly went through all of it for you and me! We thank Him!

Yes, emotions can be involved and often are, but is not limited to emotions. We must choose to love whether we feel it or not. *John 3:16 NIV, "For God so loved the world that He gave His one and Only Son."* God chose to love us. God did not consider our rejection of Him, our disobedience, and hardened hearts. The Bible says, He suffered the cross! This is why God commands us to love our enemies and bless those that persecute us? We have nor will have to go through what Jesus suffered for us!

I have seen how love or good feelings come afterwards but it is not based on how good that person is to you. If that were the case, we would not love nor pray for too many people. Remembering what they did to us would keep us from loving them. It is hard to hate someone you are praying for on a consistent basis. People naturally allow a mistaken perception of an individual to keep you from choosing to love that person. For example, if we perceive wrong things about a person, it will affect how we relate or do not relate to them. If you perceive the person dislikes you or has wronged you, most likely you will respond the same way. This naturally affects whether we choose to love or pray for them. God's love has absolutely nothing to do with perception. It is unconditional. His love is not just based on feelings or contingent upon what an individual has done or not done. He simply chooses to love us.

We can have the heart of God, seeing the need to win souls and then disciple. God tells us it is wise to win souls. You need to use wisdom in training and teaching them what we have learned from the Lord. So, they may train and teach someone else.

As we grow in Christ, we will conform to His image. Part of His image is compassion for others. Whenever Jesus was about to perform a miracle, He first had compassion on them. If our hearts are not open to a person's cry, we will miss the need they have, because we are failing to see that person through God's eyes and see there is a lost soul. Wrongly, at times, we concentrate on their outer appearances. Like how they dress or what they did wrong in the past or whose family they belong to that does not seem to fit in. We must see there is a need. Christ can fill any need!

In *Matthew 8:2-3,* a man with leprosy, who was unclean could not be touched according to Jewish Law (no one could come in contact with him or they would become contaminated, and become unclean themselves), lifted up his voice and cried to Jesus from a distance, *"Lord, if thou wilt, thou canst make me clean. And Jesus put forth his hand, and touched him saying, I will, be thou clean. And immediately his leprosy was cleansed." KJV* Jesus was moved with compassion toward the man with leprosy and touched him. It's not just an emotion but a compassion that flows through us. The person is touched by the love of God and it blesses that individual.

Forgiveness is also important for discipleship. This is a lesson I continue to make every effort to be taught to walk in. It can be difficult because you learn forgiveness through suffering hurt, pain and lots of rejection and more rejection! It is definitely a process forgiving or releasing a person of all offense and treating them as if they have done nothing wrong in the first place. We have to give up all rights we think we might have in holding that person guilty, because we really have no rights at all!

When we fail to release or forgive that person, we are in fact condemning them and this not only wrong but hinders our relationship with Christ. Christ has every right to punish us and hold us accountable for our sins, but He offers forgiveness to all who will receive Him. Judgment is of the Lord's! We cannot condemn anyone! God says "if we do not forgive others, He will not forgive us.

I remember one time when someone was particularly difficult, and I was frustrated with that person. God spoke to me and said, "be merciful." Mercy is holding back something you perceive that person as deserving of. In God's case, it means holding back His wrath or anger. In our case, it means holding back the inclinations of the flesh, or to give a person a piece of our minds and giving up our rights to retaliate. God is saying, don't! Look at all the times

He has been merciful to us and blessed us anyway. We need that same merciful attitude towards others. Remember how much we have been forgiven of and the abundant Grace God has dealt to us. The Bible tells us in *Matthew 5:7 KJV, blessed are the merciful, for they shall obtain mercy.* We need mercy in our lives often and when we are merciful to others, God sees that. When we need it, God gives it back to us. For the same measure we give mercy, it shall be given back to us.

Too many times we lead someone to Christ and have no more dealings with that person. We have won them now what? Christ is telling us that after winning comes teaching. They need to gain knowledge just like our Savior has graced us with knowledge. If you are not a teacher, then lead them to your church and introduce them to teachers, all the while, you, who led them, need to continue to check on their well-being.

You may be thinking, now that I understand more about discipleship, where do I begin? Good question! The answer is to begin right you are. **First** in your home. You may have family members who do not know Christ. Start with them not preaching but in practical ways. Showing Christlike character, such as being kind, forgiving, trusting, and loving! People don't care how much you know until they know how much you care! It's an excellent opportunity to be a living epistle. A family that prays together, stays together.

*To be a **living epistle** means you are a **living**, breathing, walking letter* *of God's goodness, glory, and grace! ... In addition to worshiping the Lord and loving others, your life and business should bear witness that Christ is real and the Holy Spirit dwells within you daily.*

Second in our neighborhoods or communities. We live every day in the same surroundings and do not witness the love of Christ or make the invitation to receive salvation. One of my disciples and I have on several occasions witnessed door-to-door. Inviting them to church and giving them an invitation to know Christ personally as their Lord and Savior. What excuse will we make to the Lord in that day of standing before Him to give an account of the things we did in this life?

Third, in the marketplace or our jobs, where most of us spend the majority of our time. For almost forty hours a week, day after day, we see practically the same people and never witness. We have to ask ourselves, how real is Christ to us? If we are afraid or ashamed, are we really sure we are in the faith ourselves? We seldom offer the hope that is available to a dying world. We tend to think a homeless person is the only one in need of encouragement or hope. No, people on your job or business and your family. The very ones you come in contact with at the supermarket.

I've had many short meaningful conversations with people who stop me in the grocery store! Sometimes, you can feel uncomfortable and are fearful of what people may think if we talk about the Lord. I've heard many say it is a private matter or that everybody has their right to worship separately. You do indeed but, Christ has called all

Believer's to be unified. Christ has commanded us to go into the world and tell others about Himself and His power to heal save and deliver. To proclaim, the hope in Christ Jesus and that they don't want to miss the opportunity in this life to choose this Hope. Know this, if you die in your sins, you will go to hell for all eternity. There is no reprieve and the only relief you will get is Judgment Day, only for God to send you back into Hell after judging, saying, "depart from me, I never knew you."

Lastly, God has called us to tell about Him to the Nations! You may not personally go to a particular place, but you can support those who do go. There are opportunities for prayer partners, donations or sending gifts. So much we can do and are commanded to do by God, and we have such a short time!

Personally speaking, I have taught many but only a few became my disciples, those who remain with you. Some will choose to depart. Whether or not you disciple an individual, you can plant seeds or words of encouragement to bless their life. But there are many opportunities, if you just look around and open your heart and life to fit someone in! Don't worry about who will receive what you are saying or think you are a complete idiot. What makes you successful is your faithfulness to try! God so loved the world that He sent His Only Son because He saw people who were lost. He saw dying people. Lost without a Savior.

Matthew 9:37 NIV, "The harvest is plentiful, but the workers are few."

The meaning of this scripture is not of grain but of souls for God!

One of the great things about the Christian life is that it isn't just me or you talking to someone and sharing things from our own ability, but God Himself comes and lives on the inside of us. He begins to speak through us and flow through us if we let Him. We have gifts of the Holy Spirit flowing through us. God has put supernatural ability within every single one of us. You may not feel it, you may not be aware of it, but this is a promise of God's Word. It is just receiving from God and beginning to apply these principles in your life.

We are to follow Christ's example, praying each day for people we may come in contact with. Seeking God on what to say and what is the purpose for the encounter. Does God want us to lay hands on them, just pray or give an encouraging word without praying. If we get into this habit of what Jesus did, we will be ready when God brings someone across our path. As Jesus went looking for His disciples, we are to as God leads, go befriend a person if He tells us to. Not to wait for someone to come to us but to go in search of them.

Praying at all times because the people are all around us! So many want answers and are ready to listen! But you will not know who until you share! The Harvest is plentiful! Allow God to use you today!

Chapter 17

A Life of Prayer

I've heard it said many times, "Prayer changes things!" It certainly does! God promises us in His Word that He hears every word that we pray to Him. Like a good parent, He is waiting, ready, and willing to listen to our worries, concerns, and needs. If we're concerned about it, God cares! Whether we are seeking forgiveness, strength, or healing, prayer provides the channel to communicate with God and receive supernatural strength and power!

The ultimate goal of prayer is developing an intimate relationship with God.

Every failure in our lives, when properly analyzed, is a prayer failure. There's not a single sin in our lives that prayer would not have avoided, or a need prayer cannot meet. It's our greatest source of untapped power! Our spiritual lives will not rise above our prayer lives. We have been deceived into believing prayer is about persuading God to release His power. Could not be further from the truth. ***We don't have to beg and plead with God to move on our behalf.***

God tells us in His word how to pray and the effects of prayers. He sent His Son Jesus, to teach the first Disciples and all Disciples today, how to pray correctly! It is not repetitive prayers where we beg and plead and then get more people to beg and plead. Trying to twist God's arm and persuade Him to care! Sounds silly doesn't it? We do it all the time! He simply says to ask in faith without doubting and you will receive! God has given every Believer the power to take authority and release His power in a situation according to His will and it shall be done. God is not holding back His power from us. This is the same lie that satan tempted Eve in the garden with. That God was holding something back and not being honest with her. No, God has given us everything that pertains to life and godliness!

Today our "intercessors" believe we, too, must stand in the gap, or mediate, between God and man. They believe we must plead with God to save the lost, to withhold His wrath from those He is ready to judge, and to be merciful to those whose needs He is unwilling to meet because of their unworthiness. Intercessory prayer today, is interceding for others but not as if God has not done anything, but with the understanding He has provided everything!

The truth is Jesus is our Mediator between God and man.

1 Timothy 2:5 NIV, *"For there is one God, and one mediator between God and men, the man Christ Jesus."*

Jesus is praying for us and standing in the gap for us to God! For this reason, God is not angry with us nor judging anyone, no matter how awful! The Bible tells us to come boldly before the throne of

God to receive help in our time of need. This is because of the covenant God has with Jesus for us.

This should cause us to pray with confidence, that if we pray the word and pray according to the will of God, we shall have what we petition. This is so easy and reassuring to know God wants to answer our prayers more than we do. But we do not know how to ask Him with that boldness but reverence a good child would give to a parent!

Our prayers should be more of asserting our authority over anything *hindering us from* the will of God! Praying, believing God has already done it! If it's the word and the will of God, why do we doubt it will happen?

God invites us to intimately connect with him through prayer, and what better way to do that than to use his own words in the Bible! And as you pray Scripture, you'll find new ways to talk to God too. When we pray the word of God, we are praying the scriptures over a given situation. For example, "no weapon formed against you shall prosper." It is scripturally sound to pray what God's word already states! We know the answer before we pray because we are coming into agreement with *what God said*. Sure, this is *God's idea* and we are simply stand with Him!

To pray according to the will of God is to pray what has already been revealed as His will. The Holy Spirit as your umpire and the word of God as your manual! God is not obligated to answer any matter apart from His will. It's wanting our lives to align with God's will more than our own desires. God's will for us is to know Him in a personal way and to live for Him. When we pray God's will for our lives, we are setting aside what we want and desire, and we're asking for what He desires instead.

We *must* learn to pray.

The following prayer quotes will help inspire and encourage your prayer life as you seek a stronger faith. "Our prayers may be awkward. Our attempts may be feeble. But since the power of prayer is in the one who hears it and not in the one who says it, our prayers do make a difference." - Max Lucado

"To be a Christian without prayer is no more possible than to be alive without breathing." - Martin Luther

"The Christian life is not a constant high. I have my moments of deep discouragement. I have to go to God in prayer with tears in my eyes, and say, 'O God, forgive me,' or 'Help me.'" - Billy Graham

"True prayer is neither a mere mental exercise nor a vocal performance. It is far deeper than that - it is spiritual transaction with the Creator of Heaven and Earth." - Charles Spurgeon

"Prayer is simply talking to God like a friend and should be the easiest thing we do each day." - Joyce Meyer

"I have been driven many times upon my knees by the overwhelming conviction that I had nowhere else to go. My own wisdom and that of all about me seemed insufficient for that day." - Abraham Lincoln

The Bible

1 John 5:14, 15 NIV, "This is the confidence we have in approaching God: that if we ask anything according to his will, he hears us. And if we know that he hears us—whatever we ask—we know that we have what we asked of him.

You will never know nor fulfill the call of God on your life without prayer. God tells us in His word, to seek Him. Seek means until you have an answer, do not cease to pray. Ceasing not meaning 24 hours a day but fervently and often!

Matthew 26:36 NIV, Jesus said to His disciples, *"sit here while I go over there and pray."*

This is your time with God and Jesus! When Jesus was on the earth, He knew the importance of time alone with the Father. He taught His disciples how to pray. Jesus is our ultimate example. He always prayed and spent time communicating with His Father, especially before making any important decisions. He did this when He chose His first Disciples. He sought direction from the Father. He desired the Father's will not His own. Since Jesus spent time with the Father and He is our perfect example, we are to follow His example. We should consult the Lord on what to do for each day for direction, and guidance.

What does the word devotional mean?

The act of being devoted. To give or apply (one's time, attention, or self) entirely to a particular activity or cause. To set apart for a specific purpose or use. Daily devotional is time spent with God and set apart each day to center your focus on Him.

In order to live in victory, prayer has to become a lifestyle for you! In order to have a relationship with God, you must pray! To know His voice and where He is leading you. To become familiar with His ways and grow in love with Him. Through my daily devotions, I have come to enjoy getting up and spending time with Father, talking and listening to Him. At times I even sing to Him. He likes to be sung to!

That is why it is so important to have personal time alone with God. Your relationship with Him cannot survive without it. If you have not had time alone with Him, I venture to say you often feel defeated and frustrated. Peace is lacking in some areas of your life! God wants to fill those areas for you! It is important to make God your top priority. Above your spouse and children. Your spouse or children cannot give you the joy and peace, which only comes through Jesus Christ. Pick a time each day you can get alone and spend communing with God through Jesus Christ. My suggestion is to start with 10 minutes. As you get more comfortable gradually increase the time. Talk to Him throughout the day and night! There is no set time, just whenever and how long you feel like it!

God will prepare you through time spent with Him for attacks of the enemy or for anything coming against you to disturb your life. Most of the time, you won't know how the Lord prepared you until afterwards!

Starting my day talking with God is an enjoyable blessing. This is the time I pray to God and always ask forgiveness for any sins I've committed. I intercede on behalf of those on my job, my family, friends, and church members. Never forget to pray for your enemies. They need forgiveness and mercy too, they need Jesus. I lift my pastor and his wife (family) to the Lord for that day and most of the time I remember to pray for our President and his cabinet and for the nation.

Again, I sing to the Lord whatever song is on my heart. Sometimes when I forget the words, the Holy Spirit will bring them to my remembrance! Usually I read at least a verse of scripture. Of course, you may read as much as you like. I would suggest at least a verse or two. To get the word in your spirit for the day and meditate on that word throughout the day. I also read from a couple of different devotionals books to further encourage myself. And don't forget to read the entire Bible as many times as you can!

Take time to not only pray and talk to God but listen to His responses. It will become easier each time, to know His voice and ways! Sometimes when struggling with trials and tribulations, I do not feel like saying much, so I just sing or praise Him. You will figure out what is best for you the more you do it. By all means, just be real to God. He knows and you cannot fool Him. So why try?

Why would you want to? We have a God who genuinely cares so we can feel comfortable being honest. In His presence is a 'safe place.'

The time in His Presence, is gratifying, leaving you confident, peaceful, and full of joy! You cannot be unchanged while in the presence of God! Devote yourself to building your relationship with the One who died so you might have life!

Pray for yourself! As you pray for others, don't neglect to cover yourself in prayers! You cannot be of much help to someone else if you are broken. For example, abusive people abuse others. They repeat the cycle. From one point of view, it doesn't make sense when a person coming from an abusive relationship, is drawn to other abusive people. When a child grows up in abuse or has had an abusive relationship; and in their adult years has a family, they will more than likely repeat the cycle with their children or others. From another perspective, you can see the cycle. Unless you are delivered, you will give out what is in you! God can only use people who are usable. The freer you are in your life; the more God can use you as an example of overcoming in that area. You are the person needing prayer most before your neighbor.

Another example, a person who lacks financial understanding and application cannot successfully lead others to achieve in their finances. Each one of us, having gifting greater than other areas and God can flow through your strengths or strong points!

Why just pray for healing for someone else and neglect to include yourself when you are afflicted? Sure, the other person may receive healing but what about you? God loves you too! It is not selfish, but you want to be your best to allow God to flow through you! God wants you well and prosperous! Don't belittle yourself. If you were the only one living, God loves you! He knows every hair strand, every thought, every desire, every failure, and everything about you! Doesn't matter about your past or your failures. If you have had a good life and have many successes, you cannot earn God's love. He just loves you! There is no one who has done everything perfectly. We all have fallen short of the glory of God! Everyone needs help from time to time, some more than others. It's okay! A little boy once told me that he believed God cared about everybody else not him. Knowing this little boy heard this false information from someone, I encouraged and reassured him that God indeed loved him. That He could love everybody else with the same amount of love he loved him! He was surprised. This little boy went on to receive the Lord Jesus as his personal Lord and Savior! Now that's good news!

You cannot know the plan of God for your life thinking you are a worm or less than nothing. To God you were and are enough to die for! To endure the Cross, the mocking, the shame, and ridicule. You were enough for Him to raise Jesus from the dead, accepting Jesus sacrifice for you. So that you may be restored back to right relationship with Him by receiving the gift He offered!

Are you broken, probably. So was I and God is still working on me. Are you a mess, possibly. Who isn't or has not been were God has done mighty works in that person. It's a new day! Wake up to the blessings of the Lord and receive His love for you now! God created a world for you to inhabit and be blessed. So, to be **blessed, means** that you have received an inheritance or something of value from someone as a sign of favor they have towards you. You have favor with God! Your inheritance is through Jesus Christ, the Son of God (*Ephesians 1*).

Jesus, when He walked on the earth, knew the importance of prayer! In fact, Jesus is our ultimate example of a life-filled prayer! He relied on His humanity not on His deity and was submitted and solely depended on God the Father for answers. He did not make any important decisions without consulting the Father. Remember, He chose His Disciples after prayer and then taught them how to pray. Prayer is communicating with God. Seeking Him for answers and expecting and listening for His response.

When Jesus was tempted by the devil in the wilderness; it was after He had prayer and fasted forty days with the Father! Prayer will strengthen you and be a channel of encouragement for God to move in your situation. Prayer invites God into your life in *any* area. The night before He was arrested, He prayed. *For Jesus to say, "I always do what I see my Father doing and I always say what my Fathers tells me to say,"* He had to know the Father's will! Only by fervent daily and throughout the day and night, praying time! Prayer is confidence that God will answer.

Mark 11:22-24 NKJV, "So Jesus answered and said to them, "Have faith in God. 23 For assuredly, I say to you, whoever says to this mountain, 'Be removed and be cast into the sea,' and does not doubt in his heart, but believes that those things he says will be done, he will have whatever he says. 24 Therefore I say to you, whatever things you ask when you pray, believe that you receive them, and you will have them."

Prayer seeks from God, asks of God, and receives from God! The power of prayer has overcome enemies (*Psalm 6:9-10*), conquered death (*2 Kings 4:3-36*), brought healing (*James 5:14-15*), and defeated demons (*Mark 9:29*). The power of prayer should never be underestimated because it draws on the glory and might of the infinitely powerful God of the universe! God, through prayer, opens eyes, changes hearts, heals wounds, and grants wisdom:

James 1:5 NIV, "If anyone lacks wisdom, let him ask of God, who gives to all liberally and without reproach, and it will be given to him."

Proverbs 4:7 NKJV, "Wisdom is the principal thing; therefore, get wisdom. And in all your getting, get understanding."

Pray for wisdom and understanding. Take for example, King Solomon. God told Solomon to build the temple; gave him wisdom. With that wisdom, He built the temple. It was as a permanent place of worship and the main center of devotion for the God of Heaven. God instructed Solomon of the detailed plan of building the temple;

similar to the case of Noah and the Ark. Solomon used the wisdom gifted to him by God to build. God provided the men to work on it and connections or partners to help him! It was magnificent! Pray for understanding or to interpret or view something in a particular way. God is not limited to any one area of your life. Whether it trying to understand your homework assignment, a job duty, or a surgical procedure in the operating room, God knows how to impart that wisdom into you to make it clear for you! After all, He created a Universe!

We are to pray without ceasing. To pray often and as needed. It would be impossible for us to pray endlessly on an individual basis but as a group or team or church, the Believers can offer prayers non-stop. Don't ever come to a point in your life where you cease to pray at all!

Chapter 18

Keep Going! Your Best is Yet to Come!

See your best days up ahead! Your current circumstances do not rule out God's miracle working power in your life! And God does not consult your past to determine your future. Your past has no value. Definitely, we can learn from our mistakes, but some people are not learning anything from focusing on the past. They just don't visit sometimes; they live in the past! They live with regrets and guilt. Others say, "Que sera, sera" meaning 'whatever will be, will be'.

Don't live in the past, thinking about mistakes and living in regrets, having guilt as your companion. ***Think of your life as a book, move forward, close one chapter and open another!*** Learn from your mistakes, but focus on your future, not on your past. Tell yourself, your future looks brighter and more amazing than ever before! I can do all things through Christ, who strengthens me! It is His strength, not mine, I depend on Him and press into His power! He sustains my comings and goings!

God has given you His supernatural, overcoming power to withstand any obstacles! ***You are an overcomer***! God never looks at your failures to evaluate your successes! God sees your end before He sees your beginning. He sees the completed work in you before you were ever born! In the book of *Psalms, God says, He knew you before you were formed in your mother's womb!* God not only saw Adam, but He saw Eve. Eve and all of mankind was inside of Adam! Therefore, He saw you being born one day! You are not a surprise to God! He intentionally created and had purpose for you!

***Philippians 3:14 NIV**, "I press on toward the goal to win the prize for which God has called me heavenward in Christ Jesus." ...* ***Philippians 3:14 NLT**, "I press on to reach the end of the race and receive the heavenly prize for which God, through Christ Jesus, is calling us."*

We are to run as if in a race; only one receives the prize but we are to run that we might obtain it! It is a race not given to the swift nor to the strong, but it is a race of pacing yourself as if in a marathon! With the resolve, you are in this for the distance!

How should you run this race? Give it all you've got; run to win! In a actual race, some have no intention of winning or finishing! Others may be intending to run but will not even begin! They just want it to be known, that they tried, or they even ran! There is another group, that will run to the finish line, even though a winner as been declared!

The Apostle Paul describes this sporting event to that of our spiritual walk in this life. Sporting events such as the Olympics, Kentucky Derby, Nascar races, Soccer, Wimbledon, and so many others require much discipline. You have to deny yourself in many ways. Foods, partying, family time, sleep; you are pushing your body, mind and whole being to train! You are training to win. In those days, they did not receive gold medals but a wreath. They ran for the mere pleasure of accomplishment!

How much more in the Kingdom of God, should we be as determined and focused? Paul said at the end of his earthly journey, he just wanted to be found faithful to God and what He had planned for him to do! Paul's focus was to receive a crown of righteousness waiting for him and everyone who is waiting for Him!

If anyone had a reason to live in the past of failures and regrets, it was Paul, who had murdered Christians and took part in others demise. After the Lord Jesus opened his eyes to what he was doing, Paul could have lived the rest of his life miserably in guilt and shame! Allowing his past to rob his future by not accepting what God said about him. What God thought about him; for God was not concerned about his past. The past was in the past in God's mind! He was forgiven!

God had a plan for Paul as He does for you! Your past could have included the vilest acts of sin, but God sees you as valuable! He sees you worthy enough to die for and save from an eternity of being lost! God still has a plan for your life! The Apostle Paul went on to write one third of the Bible as we know today! God has a unique plan just for you; cannot be compared to anyone else! He sees this plan as a perfect fit!

Some have not turned the chapter in your lives in a long time!

Still stuck on that same page of complaining and blaming others and the world. Still thinking about what happened twenty years ago in high school. There is nothing new under the sun, the Bible tells us. God is not saying it is okay to repeat the same mistakes just because someone else did. He is saying, your problems are not unique. Eve shifted the blame after the Fall in the Garden of Eden. Adam then blamed Eve and God for giving her to him. Who are you blaming for not moving forward? For not turning the page of the chapter in your life. Your parents, teacher, the government, the judicial system, your siblings, racism, or the church perhaps; the lists can go on and on! It is time to forgive and heal!

Grief vs mourning

Death, loss, and prolonged trauma are the leading causes of grief according to statistics! I would like to address this because this is the leading reason people cannot grasp what's going on in their present. Left unattended, God's plan for your life will aborted.

Grief - deep sorrow, especially that caused by someone's death.

Mourning - feel regret or sadness about (the loss or disappearance of something).

When Adam and Eve sinned in the Garden of Eden and mankind fell, their eyes were immediately opened to good and evil. Which is what God did not want. The Bible states, they knew also they were naked. Actually, they were always naked but were unaware of this. The glory of God was their covering! There was no need for cloths. They were now focused on self. God wanted them to be only focused on Him! When we focus on our losses, no matter how great, we are focused on ourselves.

Philippians 1:21 NKJV, "For to me, to live is Christ and to die is gain."

In grieving for that person is in most cases, no longer with you and if they have died, they cannot share in what you are going through. They are not aware of you or your struggles. They cannot come back to you in this earth. Particularly for a Believer who has died, the Bible tells us they have changed locations (earth to heaven) minus their earthly bodies. Nevertheless, we can take comfort that God is the righteous judge and He wants you to move on. It should be a time of rejoicing and thanksgiving to God for their being with Him! They have left this sinful world and are now in the presence of God and Jesus and all of heaven! Instead of thinking about what we have lost, think about what that person has gained! Instead, we are focused on ourselves and what we will miss. The Believer is fine and rejoicing themselves. Free from the bounds of this fallen world and free from the snares of the enemy.

Another source of grief is pride! Pride in your relationships with other people. Heated disputes and disagreements are full of pride. Pride is self-thinking and not really about the other person. You are involved with your feelings, vanity and being stuck-up. It's all about you and it will cause bitterness to take root in your life. This is a loss of something; a relationship and will cause your heart to grieve if you don't release it and allow God to heal you! God shares in His word; it is okay to grieve for the loss of someone but don't mourn too long! Time in prayer with God will answer the question, how long is' too long' this supposed to be; this will vary.

We can learn so much from reading the word of God! The Bible tells us what God thinks about grief and mourning. Grief is the initial reactions to the loss of someone. Mourning is more of the process of time after grief to adjust to that loss. To deal with grief you have to deal with self. We convince ourselves that we are mourning over the death of these people, but it's really over how it will affect us. The answer to self is shifting focus on someone else. Find someone to help, minister in the other person's situation, and you will find yourself forgetting about your own worries. You'll also discover that what you thought was so important is really not as bad. Love for another person will always overcome self.

Living in your past will only hurt you! Another very comforting thing to remember in a time of grief is that the situation is only temporary. The Bible tells us, life here is temporary! No tragedy is permanent. Even death is only a temporary separation. This is good news! But if you don't choose to allow God to heal and deliver you, the enemy will steal, kill, and destroy your life. It doesn't have to be this way!

He is not controlling the affairs (events and activities) of your life, but He is with you! Fully aware of you and caring about you. The awful thing that happened to you, almost destroying you was not from God. We do have an enemy and his job (what he does), is to steal, kill, and to destroy!

I Corinthians 2:9 AMPC, "But, on the contrary, as the Scripture says, eye has not seen and ear has not heard and has not entered into the heart of man, [all that] God has prepared (made and keeps ready) for those who love Him [who hold Him in affectionate reverence, promptly obeying Him and gratefully recognizing the benefits He has bestowed].

As a Believer trusts in God and surrenders to His will and way, God will reveal step by step His plans for you. I see that happening in my life. There were jobs I wanted and did not get but looking back I see God's hands in some open or closed doors. There were instances, later I was glad I did not get the job. Other times, I realize how the job was not a good fit, but God knew that! God is a good God and wants the best for us. He knows the right paths we should take and the seasons of our lives.

No matter what your life's challenges, hurts or failures, these cannot preclude God's plan for your life! God loves you and is able to redeem the time of your past. Be strong in the Lord and confident in God's ability to bring good out of your life to prosper you! Nothing the enemy has tried to destroy you with has worked. The fact that we are here today is evidence (proof) that our past (yesterdays) could not defeat us.

Romans 8:28 AMPC tells us, "We are assured and know that [God being a partner in their labor] all things work together and are [fitting into a plan] for good to and for those who love God and are called according to [His}design and purpose."

Therefore, it is not satan who can stop you (he can hinder you) and not God who wills to stop you, the variable is YOU! It is you who can abort the vision. You may not want to complete or obey what God has told you to do! You have power to obey or disobey and to reject or receive. To work with God or not. God's will for your life has to involve your cooperation. On God's side, He has given the invitation: whomsoever wants to come, let him come! We are called by God to do something. Not just coming to church, being a good Christian and going home. This is not what God called us to do. God wants us to serve Him! To make a difference!

Don't get stuck in the day to day rut, of going to work and coming home tired and then starting it over again. Sadly, this seems to be the normal for most people. It was for me for a long time! Until God opened my eyes! Same old rut mentality. Instead of saying "I can do all things through Christ who strengthens me," we say, "I can do nothing." I've met so many people, who live for Friday and the weekends but consider Monday as blue. Dreading going back to work. You can spend over forty hours of each week depressed because it is not Friday or the weekend. Are you only happy on these days? It is such a waste, isn't it? You are living to make money on a job you hate and feeling powerless to change the situation! Only God is able to change the situation!

Why not place your life and plans into the hand of God, who wants to increase you in every area! If you are doing nothing, nothing from nothing equals nothing. Cannot run or win a race without effort on your part. We make wrong assumptions, that God will do everything. There is no such thing as standing still. If you are not moving forward, you are going backwards. Time and years are passing you by and nothing will be accomplished. If you don't make a change, your situation will negatively change you!

Also, we should never rest in a place of satisfaction in our accomplishments. Awards, recognitions, and achievements will keep you living in the memories of your past! We must press on and not be content with our present circumstances. If we do, we will find ourselves reminiscing over the things that God did 'back in the day'. Paul was successful in many ways before the Lord changed his life. We know that Paul held Roman citizenship. He was given an outstanding education; it has been said that by the time he was twenty-one that he had earned the equivalent of two advanced academic degrees. He was an Israelite of the tribe of Benjamin and was raised a Pharisee. He studied in the Jerusalem school of Rabbi Gamaliel, one of the leading Jewish thinkers of his time.

But Paul in all his successes, surrendered them all unto the Lordship of Jesus Christ! Stating, he had not considered himself to be perfect but pressing toward the calling of God in Christ Jesus! He felt his relationship with Jesus was more important than all his education and status. That his past meant nothing without Christ! We can learn from Paul's example of how he lived his life after conversion. Your money, status and education do not mean a thing without Christ! These material things are temporary but only what you do for Christ is eternal!

Money cannot buy everything. It is a fact, some people with millions of dollars in the bank have committed suicide. It can buy a lot but not joy, peace or eternal life! Everything is subject under the Lordship of Jesus Christ and in His name! The Bible says, your education means nothing if you don't fear God; that you are foolish!

It is good to have memories of the 'back in the day,' but what testimonies to you have of what God has done recently for you? There should be a fresh word or 'Thank you Jesus' on our lips every day! Relationship with God and Jesus is not an event or memory; it is a lifestyle! *Live for more accomplishments!*

What you are holding so tightly in your hand, how do you know if you let it go, God can't replace it with something far more beautiful. Saul's education, his background as a Pharisee, his Roman citizenship, and his unflagging zeal all contributed to his success as a missionary! An important lesson, God doesn't do away with your giftings but includes them for good things and for His purposes!

The gifts and calling of God are not unto repentance meaning they are God-given, and God uses them for His glory! The problem is we use them not to give God glory but for our own purposes and agenda. A Christian should want to allow God to flow through our gifts to bless others as well!

Like Paul, we can recognize and hear the voice of God telling us His plan for our lives! His goal now in life was to apprehend that for which he was apprehended by Jesus Christ. He realized that when the Lord apprehended him, that the Lord had a plan for his life. His goal now was to accomplish that plan. For each of us the only thing that really counts in life is to apprehend that for which God created us. We have only one life before death, it will soon pass, only what's done for Christ will last! The most fulfilling moment in life is when you suddenly realize that God used you to accomplish His purpose! To realize that God's hand was on your life guiding you to fulfill His purpose!

We *picture* the marathon race; with you approaching the finish line, and you digging deep inside for that extra kick that might win the race! Press toward the mark! The reward is so great! "The high calling of God in Christ Jesus!" Amen

Conclusion

Expected End

The prophet, Jeremiah came with a message of comfort: *"I know the thoughts that I think toward you, saith the LORD, thoughts of peace, and not of evil, to give you an expected end."* It was a message of hope. How wonderful that our God wants us to have peace. He genuinely wants us to be safe, well, and happy.

Your life can be limited and circumstances unfavorable right now. You may have been abused, rejected, lonely and confused. Yet God wants you to have a more substantial and prosperous future. God has a hopeful end for His people.

God's plan is salvation! What is salvation? Knowing God and Jesus, whom He sent. It is healing, prosperity, deliverance, and eternal life in one glorious marvelous package! God wants to bring you back to the reason He created the Garden of Eden! The book of Revelation details this is where the Believers are headed in the end! When God speaks, His word does not come back void but is sent out to accomplish what He said. Man may have messed up the original intent of God's plan for us, but God will have the last word!

The ultimate plan of God for mankind is the same. How God

brings this plan fulfilled in our individual lives is that which varies. A great deal hinges on ***timing*** and ***your cooperation***. The enemy has NO power to stop you from being born again or reaching heaven. If this is your will, you can have it! God wills it, so let it be done!

In Jesus Name!

Receive Jesus

Personal Invitation to Salvation

Choosing to receive Jesus Christ as your Lord and Savior is the most important decision you'll ever make!

Romans 10:9, 10 NKJV, "that if you confess with your mouth the Lord Jesus and believe in your heart that God has raised Him from the dead, you will be saved. For with the heart one believes unto righteousness, and with the mouth confession is made unto salvation.

By His grace, God has already done everything to provide salvation. Your part is simply to believe and receive.

The very moment you commit your life to Jesus Christ, the truth of His Word instantly comes to pass in your spirit. Now that you're born again, there's a brand-new you!

If you prayed this prayer and have received Jesus in your heart, you need to be connected to a local church with fellow Believers to keep you encouraged, strengthened learning in the faith. Ask God to show you the right church to attend. Get into a good Bible teaching Bible study and do not neglect your personal devotional time with God.

Receive the Holy Spirit

As His child, your loving heavenly Father wants to give you the supernatural power you need to live this new life.

> *"For every one that asks receives; and he that seeks finds; and to him that knocks it shall be opened... If ye...know how to give good gifts unto your children: how much more shall your heavenly Father give the Holy Spirit to them that ask him?"*
>
> *Luke 11:10,13 KJV*

All you have to do is ask, believe, and receive! Pray, *Father, I recognize my need for Your power to live this new life. Please fill me with Your Holy Spirit. By faith, I receive Him right now! Thank You for baptizing me. Holy Spirit, you are welcome in my life.*

Congratulations! Now you're filled with God's supernatural power. Some syllables from a language you don't recognize will rise up from your heart to your mouth. (See *1 Cor. 14:14*.) As you speak them out loud by faith, you're releasing God's power from within and building yourself up in the Spirit. (See v. 4.) You can do this whenever and wherever you like.

It doesn't really matter whether you felt anything or not when you prayed to receive the Lord and His Spirit. If you believed in your heart that you received, then God's Word promises you did. "Therefore, I say unto you, Whatever things you ask, when you pray, believe that you receive them, and you shall have them" (*Mark 11:24*). God always honors His Word; believe it!

About the Author

Marguerite Wafula has been born-again for 48 years. Through this relationship with God, been happily married to her husband, Moses! They currently live in Greensboro NC where they are Pastors and oversee GraceWay Church International in Kenya and Uganda. A local church is in the plan. She and her husband have founded Walking by Faith Ministry International, where they teach and preach, with an emphasizes on Relationship with God, Finances and Healing! She and her husband have founded a Missions School in Kenya and have 25 missionaries. Marguerite has traveled to Dominion Republic and Africa.

Website: www.walkingbyfaithministry.org

Blog: www.wakeuptohope.blog

You can write or email us at:

Walking by Faith Ministry, Po Box 8182, Greensboro, NC 27419.

walkingbyfaith4611@gmail.com.

Printed in the United States
By Bookmasters